HowExpert Amusement Parks and Roller Coasters

101+ Tips to the Best Amusement Parks, Roller Coasters, and Theme Parks in the World

HowExpert with Noah Granger

Copyright HowExpert™
www.HowExpert.com

For more tips related to this topic, visit HowExpert.com/amusementparks.

Recommended Resources

- HowExpert.com – Quick 'How To' Guides on All Topics from A to Z by Everyday Experts.
- HowExpert.com/free – Free HowExpert Email Newsletter.
- HowExpert.com/books – HowExpert Books
- HowExpert.com/courses – HowExpert Courses
- HowExpert.com/clothing – HowExpert Clothing
- HowExpert.com/membership – HowExpert Membership Site
- HowExpert.com/affiliates – HowExpert Affiliate Program
- HowExpert.com/jobs – HowExpert Jobs
- HowExpert.com/writers – Write About Your #1 Passion/Knowledge/Expertise & Become a HowExpert Author.
- HowExpert.com/resources – Additional HowExpert Recommended Resources
- YouTube.com/HowExpert – Subscribe to HowExpert YouTube.
- Instagram.com/HowExpert – Follow HowExpert on Instagram.
- Facebook.com/HowExpert – Follow HowExpert on Facebook.
- TikTok.com/@HowExpert – Follow HowExpert on TikTok.

Publisher's Foreword

Dear HowExpert Reader,

HowExpert publishes quick 'how to' guides on all topics from A to Z by everyday experts.

At HowExpert, our mission is to discover, empower, and maximize everyday people's talents to ultimately make a positive impact in the world for all topics from A to Z...one everyday expert at a time!

All of our HowExpert guides are written by everyday people just like you and me, who have a passion, knowledge, and expertise for a specific topic.

We take great pride in selecting everyday experts who have a passion, real-life experience in a topic, and excellent writing skills to teach you about the topic you are also passionate about and eager to learn.

We hope you get a lot of value from our HowExpert guides, and it can make a positive impact on your life in some way. All of our readers, including you, help us continue living our mission of positively impacting the world for all spheres of influences from A to Z.

If you enjoyed one of our HowExpert guides, then please take a moment to send us your feedback from wherever you got this book.

Thank you, and we wish you all the best in all aspects of life.

Sincerely,

BJ Min
Founder & Publisher of HowExpert
HowExpert.com

PS...If you are also interested in becoming a HowExpert author, then please visit our website at HowExpert.com/writers. Thank you & again, all the best!

Table of Contents

Chapter 5: World-class attractions (that aren't roller coasters) that you should also add to the bucket list

Chapter 6: Other Aspects of Theme Parks.116

Chapter 7: The Visit Itself! 121

Chapter 1: Admission

Here's a quick childhood memory of mine; perhaps you'll recall a similar memory to this one. I was sitting in the backseat of my parents' Honda Accord, going about 70 miles per hour on Interstate 5. *"Disneyland Dr., Exit Only,"* read the green freeway sign overhead. As a kid, nothing could *possibly* surpass the excitement of visiting the "Happiest Place on Earth." My young, naïve self could not understand why my parents weren't as excited as I was about the day, even when they had to give the lady at the parking booth $20. After the "this cost for parking is highway robbery" or the "Mickey Mouse must have raised the prices to park to take Minnie on more dates" jokes, they finally found a parking spot. For those who have been to Disneyland before, you know the drill from here. You take the elevator down and eventually find yourself walking over to the tram lines. It's the first of many lines. This is a line you must savor; it might be the shortest line of the day. Anywho, after a tram ride and then a walk through Downtown Disney, you finally reach the entrances of Disney's California Adventure and Disneyland. For my family, this day was a Disneyland day.

We entered through the gates and were greeted with the Disneyland Railroad, a classic. My parents were enticed to get us to immediately get on the train, probably because the line was short. My brother and I responded with an opposing "No, no, no... we're going to Space Mountain." Instead, we were walking through the charming, colorful, and forced perspective of Mainstreet, USA. Marching bands were tooting their horns in formations, horse carriages were transporting families who were already tired and sweaty, and the Gibson Girl Ice Cream Parlor was emitting its enticing smells of... well, of Ice Cream.

Tip 1: If the park you're attending has a horse carriage for transportation (*cough cough Disneyland), let the horse take you. You'll get a break from walking, and it's fun.

After taking a right turn, we head into Tomorrowland. A section of the park (that quite frankly, in my opinion, needs to be updated) that presents guests with representations of futuristic visions and fantasies. Star Tours had a line of ninety minutes, but we pretended not to see that. Unfortunately, that was a precursor to the two-hour line of Space Mountain. Immediately, we acted as if this was a surprise, even though it wasn't. Therefore, we pivoted to the "Fast Pass get me out of jail free card," and each got Fast Passes instead of waiting in the two-hour line. Without this safety net, we knew it was time to wait in the real lines. Despite the day being filled with these long lines, expensive turkey legs, and germ-infested bathrooms, we were also getting another experience. We were immersed into the tales of Fantasyland (getting *It's a Small World* stuck in our heads, again); being plunged into the search for Jack Sparrow in *Pirates of the Caribbean* and fancying myself as "edgy" for looking into the forbidden eyes of Mara while riding *Indiana Jones* in Adventureland. However, we were too cool to go to Toontown at that point. This was a sad day for our parents because we were growing up. Disneyland also had some roller coasters. They may not have been as thrilling as the scream machines they had a few hours down the five at Six Flags, but they were well-themed and likely a mountain. Ironically enough, the one roller coaster at the park that was not named after a mountain was still indeed a mountain. *Matterhorn* jolted us around the first tubular steel track; Splash *Mountain* soaked us with water while *Thunder Mountain* dried us off with its windy layout. Our day, or at this point night, was capped off with the Fireworks Spectacular.

Tip 2: If the park you're attending has a nighttime show or "spectacular" that attracts a lot of guests, then consider hopping in line for popular attractions during the show (that is, if you don't mind missing the show). There's also nothing cooler than being on a roller coaster during a firework show!

As per usual, we were sticklers for foot traffic and decided to watch from the parking structure to beat the crowds and make it home at a reasonable hour. Other families stayed to watcaaah on Mainstreet, but likely these families waited a long time sitting on the curb of Mainstreet, which gave their kids more wiggle room to convince their parents to buy something at the gift shop for them. Or maybe it's the other way around; I'm not sure since I would already be in the parking structure during this hypothetical situation. Nevertheless, this was the end of a "magical" Disney day. Whether or not you've been to Disneyland, I'm sure you've had some sort of theme park or amusement park experience like this one. It may be a different kind of park than Disneyland; perhaps it's more geared towards thrills and teenagers. Maybe it's Universal Studios, which in that case, your day was likely filled with simulators where you look at screens with 3D glasses. This book is written to help you understand all things theme/amusement parks. We'll discuss the best park destinations, roller coasters to add to your bucket list, and tips and tricks for when you go to the park. We'll also be sprinkling tips (107 of them, to be exact) throughout the book that should enhance your next trip to a park. By the end of this read, you should be an expert on each of the various aspects of these parks, their attractions, and your next visit. Speaking of parks, let's start there. There are numerous types of parks, each of which is looking to target a different demographic. I want to begin this introduction by differentiating theme parks from amusement parks. People typically use each term interchangeably, but they are not interchangeable. They are not terms to be conflated with one another. Allow me to share why.

Theme Parks vs. Amusement Parks (Yes, there is a difference)

Theme parks and amusement parks are different in how they aim to entertain their guests, and they have differing objectives. Understanding the difference between the two is relatively easy, as it's literally in the names "Theme" park and "Amusement" park. Theme parks may be a *type* of amusement park, but they offer something entirely different for guests. Theme parks have the objective to immerse their guests into a storyline, a fantasy in many instances. An obvious example that comes to mind is Disneyland. When guests visit Disneyland, guests are entering the places in which their favorite fictional movie series take place. We'll use the new Star Wars Galaxy's Edge, for example. Disneyland boasts this land to be "an-out-of -this-world" where guests live their own Star Wars experience on the planet Batuu. The topography of the rock formations looks to part, and the landscaping and architecture of the various building are fully themed and look straight out of the movies. Even down to the slightest detail, every nook and cranny is detailed to the movie it depicts. The full-scale Millennium Falcon is the clear centerpiece, and guests can also ride the Millennium Falcon on *Smugglers Run,* build their own light saber, and drink at Oga's Catina.

Rise of the Resistance is another attraction you may have heard of. It made our "World class attractions (that aren't roller coasters) that you should also add to the "bucket list" section of the book. So we'll rave about this particular ride later in the book. A rather apparent observation about each ride or themed section of Disneyland is that there is a storyline where the guests in some way play an important role in the story or are thrown right into the action. This is what a "Theme" park is. Now let's take a trip down Interstate 5, from Anaheim to Valencia. It'll probably be an hour and a half drive. Valencia is home to Six Flags Magic Mountain, a 262-acre-sized roller coaster enthusiast sanctuary. This is an "Amusement" park.

Tip 3: Always consider purchasing a season pass to your local park in the instance where you are going for just the day. Typically passes pay for themselves after just a few visits, which makes the pass a much better deal than a one-day admission.

As I mentioned, theme parks are, in fact, amusement parks, but to understand the difference, we must differentiate the two into two categories. What is quite apparent to visitors of the park is that there is less of an effort when it comes to theming the various lands. The rides have more of a goal to thrill riders and scare the living daylights out of them rather than making them feel as if they are helping Buzz Lightyear defeat Emperor Zurg. Six Flags Magic Mountain boasts more roller coasters than any other amusement park. By the end of the year 2022, they'll be the first park to have 20 coasters. As roller coaster enthusiasts say, they also are home to an impressive "lineup" of roller coasters.

Tip 4: A "lineup" at an amusement park refers to the park's collection of roller coasters. Coaster enthusiasts expect a lineup to offer different types and models of roller coasters that offer different kinds of thrills to their guests.Think of this lineup similar to a baseball or basketball team; different players (or roller coasters) fulfill different roles in the team (or the park). Kiddie rides may not be exciting, but they are necessary to the team because they offer younger kids an opportunity to ride. The same could be said for family coasters (moderate thrills) and scream machines (self-explanatory). The roller coaster enthusiast community speaks a different language at times.

Although Six Flags Magic Mountain attempts in a few of its attractions to add some theming to their rides, the majority of rides have little to no storyline or theme. The theming that is present also tends to be lazy or lacks substance. When visiting amusement parks, visitors usually have the expectation that their experience will be more about the thrills and screams of rides rather than being immersed in their favorite movie or series. Amusement parks that brand themselves as theme parks are deceitful; never allow a Six Flags chained park to convince you that their DC or Bugs Bunny-themed attractions will actually immerse you into some sort of narrative (unless it's Six Flags Fiesta Texas, this park, in particular, is quite excellent in theming).

Nevertheless, I will concede that Six Flags Magic Mountain has, over the years, invested more into theming the new lands and sections of the park. It is true that some amusement parks do have *some* theming. Whether we define a park as a "Theme" park or an "Amusement" park comes down to how elaborate that theming is and how much it plays a role in the visitor's experience. Before we move forward, I want to mention this: during my visits to Six Flags Magic Mountain, I always come across advertisements in the park, even on the ride trains and vehicles. This is another clear indicator that the park is an amusement park because park management clearly couldn't care less about theming in this instance. There are also some parks in which it may be up to your objective opinion whether it is a theme park or an amusement park. I suppose you could almost consider this a spectrum if it's not always apparent to you whether a park is a theme park or an amusement park because a park could find itself somewhere in between. However, in most cases, it's quite obvious if it's one or the other.

You should be aware of the various theme park chains (and how knowing these chains will better prepare you for your theme park experience).

Now that we've distinguished the difference between theme parks and amusement parks, let's review some of the park chains and how understanding the different chains of parks will impact the expectations of your visit; if you do indeed know the chain that the park your visiting belongs to.

- **Six Flags Entertainment Corporation:** (notable parks: Six Flags Magic Mountain, Six Flags Great Adventure, Six Flags Great America, Six Flags Mexico, La Ronde, Six Flags Over Texas).

What to expect: Yes, I did mention advertisements on ride trains and lazy theming that lacks substance. I did not mention the overly priced microwave food they serve or the gum you may or may not find under the table. But I must emphasize that visitors can usually bear these unfortunate aspects of their visit because they are not the main draw.

Tip 5: If you're going to a Six Flags park, consider the possibility of having your meals at a nearby fast-food place or restaurant. You'll get a better value for what you pay for. The only loss in this instance would be convenience because you'd need to leave a re-enter the park.

If you attend a Six Flags chained park, prepare to be thrilled in most circumstances. Six Flags dedicates itself to consistently opening and building new major thrill rides. They are the thrill seeker's chain. The unfortunate reality with Six Flags parks is they tend to prioritize thrills over everything when considering how they allocate their funds. Thrills over theming, thrills over cleanliness, thrills over food quality, and thrills over landscaping (in many instances but not all). There are a few exceptions (like Six Flags Fiesta Texas, which has excellent theming and is considering one of the cleaner Six Flags parks). You'll also come across parks like Six Flags Discovery Kingdom, which has a collection of animals (even sea creatures), and Six Flags Great Adventure, which is home to a Safari.

Tip 6: As someone (personally speaking), who is all about going on roller coasters when attending a park, I'd still recommend that you check out the animals or the safari if, in fact, the park does offer this unique feature; even for the purpose of letting you and your party's food settle in your stomach before going on another thrill ride.

Something to note is in 2021, a new CEO of Six Flags was hired, Selim A Bassoul. It appears that their business model may be changing as the season pass and ticket prices are increasing. Six Flags has been known to be a "discount chain" and has strived to be affordable for everyday day people (unlike Disney parks, where they charge an arm and a leg). It might be so that the corporation may be looking to invest more in improving the quality of the park and investing more in the food options, shows, landscaping, and cleanliness. This also would indicate that they may take a step back in the frequency of major thrill ride investments, but perhaps this may improve the overall experience for guests. We'll just have to see what happens there.

- **Merlin Entertainment Groups:** (notable parks: Alton Towers, Heide Park, LEGOLAND parks, Gardaland)

What to expect: Merlin Entertainment Groups is quite an impressive chain. Their parks are elaborately themed, even the roller coasters in many instances. And some of these roller coasters are no family rides. Instead, they are detailed and intricately themed high-speed thrilling roller coasters. When you attend a Merlin chained park, expect good landscaping, clean bathrooms, and well-rounded roller coaster lineups (usually, there are exceptions). Merlin also owns parks like LEGOLAND, and in this instance, if you attend LEGOLAND, you are probably taking kids between the age groups of infants to preteens. There may be no high-speed thrill coaster, but you will come across the perfect selection of Lego-themed attractions as well as family-oriented rides that will keep your younger kids well entertained for the whole day. Merlin also owns parks such as Chessington World of

Adventures (located in London), an animal-themed park that (surprise, surprise) has a collection of animals.

Tip 7: Merlin offers an Annual pass for ALL their UK parks for just 89 euros. I'm no advertiser, but in my opinion, that's a great deal. Alton Towers alone could sell that deal for me.

- **SeaWorld Entertainment Inc:** (notable parks: SeaWorld Orlando, SeaWorld San Diego, SeaWorld San Antonio, Busch Gardens Williamsburg, Busch Gardens Tampa)

What to expect: This may come as no surprise: you can expect to see animals at SeaWorld parks. SeaWorld parks, specifically, obviously are known to host sea animals, and both Busch Gardens parks have their own unique collection of terrestrial animals. In addition, the Busch Gardens parks specifically have excellent landscaping and theming. For example, Busch Gardens Williamsburg is themed to Europe and is regarded as one of (if not the most) beautiful parks in the United States, which is ironic. At Busch Gardens, you can expect a clean park with excellent food and a highly respected collection of roller coasters, some of which are for thrill seekers, and other moderate thrill coasters that the whole family can enjoy. Although the SeaWorld parks are currently expanding their thrill rides collection, the Orlando park specifically boasts a few impressive B&M manufactured roller coasters.

Tip 8: B&M roller coasters tend to have a loud roar (the track) while the ride vehicle runs its course through the layout. In a few instances, parks have requested sand to be filled in the track or supported with sand. This dampens the noise of the ride vehicle while the ride is running. Silver Bullet at Knott's Berry Farm and Fury 325 at Carowinds are a few examples of rides that have received this treatment.

- **Cedar Fair Entertainment Co:** (notable parks: Cedar Point, Kings Islands, Carowinds, Knott's Berry Farm, Canada's Wonderland)

What to expect: Cedar Fair parks, like the Six Flags chain, are very thrill coasters oriented. Cedar Point specifically is widely considered as one, if not the best amusement park in the world if, in fact, roller coasters are your priority. You can expect a step up in food, cleanliness, and atmosphere with the majority of Cedar Fair parks as compared to Six Flags. For that reason, Cedar Fair parks will typically charge more for admission. But obviously, this is no blanket statement; that isn't always true. Nevertheless, Cedar Fair parks tend to offer a good lineup of coasters at most of their parks. Although the theming isn't typically that great, I'd say Cedar Fair and Six Flags are generally even in that department (except for Knott's Berry Farm, which many still consider to be a "Theme" park).

- **Universal Studios Parks and Resorts:** (notable parks: Islands of Adventure, Universal Studios Hollywood, Universal Studios Orlando, Universal Studios Japan, Universal Studios Singapore)

What to expect: Universal parks bring something unique to its guests. What more could you expect from a chain owned by NBC Universal other than magnificently themed lands like *The Wizarding World of Harry Potter*, where visitors will walk the streets of Diagon Alley and to the village of Hogsmeade? Guests at the Orlando location can ride *Hagrid's Magical Creatures Motorbike Adventure,* and both parks have the world-class dark ride, *Harry Potter and the Forbidden Journey,* which we'll discuss later in this book.

Tip 9: The Butterbeer is a must if you ever visit The Wizarding World of Harry Potter.

At Universal parks, you'll come across many motion-based dark rides, most of which are excellent. From my experiences, the parks tend to be clean, and the food is above average. Universal parks are outstanding in terms of the atmosphere at their parks, probably for obvious reasons. A few of their parks are also host to excellent roller coasters, especially Islands of Adventure, which is home to *The Incredible Hulk,* as well as *Velocicoaster,* which we'll also talk about later in this book. One downside to these parks would have to be the admission price. Universal pours a lot of money into their investments with the parks/attractions, and it shows.

Tip #10: Universal Studios Hollywood offers "The World-Famous Studio Tour," which many consider will make your price of admission worth it alone. There is nothing else like this attraction. You get to go behind the scenes to the Universal backlot, where you will see the sets of Back to the Future, Jaws, Psycho (the Bates Motel), and New York and western streets in which you more than likely will recognize that you've watched something that was filmed there. I could dedicate a whole chapter to this book, raving about all the unique aspects of this experience that make it such a "must ride."

- **Walt Disney Parks and Resorts:** (notable parks: Disneyland, Tokyo Disney Sea, Epcot, Disney's Magic Kingdom, ... eh, you've heard of all of them)

What to expect: Chances are, you already know what to expect from a Disney park. You can expect an expensive day, with expensive food and expensive parking. Nevertheless, you will have a world-class experience complete with innovative dark rides, well-themed roller coasters, and of course, everyone loves *Dumbo,* and if you can stomach it, the teacups. Tokyo Disney Sea is an incredible destination that goes below the radar. I'll talk about this park a bit more extensively later in the book. Epcot is also a unique park that showcases different parts of the world. It's very well done and is my personal favorite park that Disneyworld has to offer.

Tip 11: If you ever have the opportunity to visit Epcot, be sure to keep an empty stomach. The food is excellent, and considering the world showcase: it's also diverse in what you can try. Something else that makes this all the more immersive was, when I visited Epcot, the people that work in the various parts of the world showcase are actually from that country that is being showcased because of their Cultural Exchange Program.

When you visit a Disney park, you know it will be clean. It will have good smells, and there will always be an atmosphere fitting to the land or world the park is trying to immerse its guests into. There is so much lore and history to these parks as well, which also leaves room to learn and be a part of history. Walt Disney said, "Disneyland will never be completed. It will continue to grow as long as there is imagination left in the world."

Now that we've covered these major chains let's review a few of the smaller ones you may come across.

- **Herschend Family Entertainment Co:** (notable parks: Dollywood, Silver Dollar City)

What to expect: This chain owns a lot of water parks as well, but parks such as Dollywood and Silver Dollar City are home to world-class roller coasters, incredible cuisine, clean paths, and excellent landscaping, and their parks don't quite break the bank *as* badly as Disney parks will.

- **Parques Reunidos:** (notable parks: Kennywood, Lake Compounce, Miribilandia)

What to expect: I waited to discuss this chain because I'm not entirely sure how to approach this one. Their parks are quite different from one another, so when visiting one of their parks, your experience will differ on a park-by-park basis. They also own a lot of smaller parks, zoos, water parks, and Boomers. Their major parks are home to large-scale thrill coasters, and Lake Compounce is home to *Boulder Dash,* a bucket list to ride wooden coaster of mine, which has a lot of airtime. A few of their parks in Europe, such as Movie Park, Germany, and Parque Warner Madrid, are definite theme parks with various movie-themed lands, dark rides, and coasters.

Tip 12: If airtime is something you're craving, be sure to leave a few inches of space between you and the lap bar.

Tip 13 Airtime is another valuable piece of lingo you'll want to know in order to fit in with other roller coaster enthusiasts. Airtime is that weightless feeling of negative G's in which your lap is pushing up on the lap bar, and you feel as if you're coming out of your seat. From the steep drops to airtime hills, airtime is a rather uncomfortable yet addicting sensation that ride companies such as B&M, Intamin, and RMC have mastered delivering.

- **Overseas Chinese Town Enterprises:** (notable parks: all the Happy Valley parks)

What to expect: This chain is relatively young and currently has three new parks under construction. Nevertheless, this chain offers much of what roller coasters enthusiasts in China can access, as their parks offer high thrill coasters and thrills.

- **Compagnie des Alpes Family Recreation**: (notable parks: Walibi World)

What to expect: I see this chain as a less exciting European Cedar Fair. Walibi Holland is a pretty exciting park, though; they are home to a few sweet steel coasters. That's as much as I can say.

Although we didn't quite go over *all* the various theme park chains, chances are your local park is owned by one of these. There are, however, a few family-owned parks out there as well, like Knoebles, Lagoon Amusement Park, Blackpool Pleasure Beach, Chimelong Paradise, Europa Park, Holiday World, and Djus Sommerland. Each of these parks is unique from one another. For example, Europa Park is widely considered one of the prettiest parks in the world, and the coaster collection isn't too shabby either.

All in all, your experience at the park is undoubtedly impacted by who owns the park. Hopefully, you've found this information useful, as well as the tips that will be continuously sprinkled throughout the book. Now that you know the different types of parks and park chains, it is time to go even more in-depth. In the next chapter, we'll be reviewing the different types of rides that you will be destined to run into for your next visit.

Chapter Review

- There is a difference between "Theme Parks" and "Amusement Parks," Theme parks are a type of amusement park. Theme parks aim to immerse their guests with themed lands, rides, and attractions. On the other hand, amusement parks tend to be lazy with theming and have more of an objective to thrill their guests above all else.
- Understanding the various chains of parks will better help you understand how your experience will be. For example, Disney or Universal parks tend to favor a family experience, while Six Flags or Cedar Fair parks are typically looking to thrill teenagers and young adults.
- You should try Butterbeer if you find yourself in the *Wizarding World of Harry Potter*.
- There are also numerous family-owned and run parks. These tend to generally be very good parks (sometimes even free parking) with a certain charm to them.

Chapter 2: Rides

Neither theme parks nor amusement parks are theme parks or amusement parks without their selection of rides. Rides are the reason people will pay a hefty price for tickets and then spend hours in line waiting.

Tip 14: If the park you're visiting has an app, many of them have a feature that gives a live stream of wait times for each ride. Be sure to take advantage of this if, in fact, you can.

We each can think of our personal favorite rides, but do you know what type of ride it is? If it's a roller coaster, which model? Here, we'll do an overview of the different kinds of rides that you'll likely come across on your next visit.

Roller coasters

Typically, these are the main attractions of a park—tall supports, a set of tracks, and the sounds of screaming. There are numerous types of coaster models. Here is a rundown of the types of roller coasters:

Hyper coaster: A hyper coaster is any roller coaster with a height above 200 feet.

Tip 15: The first ever hyper coaster was Magnum XL200. The name "hyper coaster" was invented by Arrow Dynamics and Cedar Point upon this release. *B&M (the company we've mentioned earlier) is known for creating airtime-filled hypercoasters with a steep drop, floater and ejector airtime hills, and an out and back layout (in most cases).*

Tip 16: Ejector vs. floater airtime is some more coaster enthusiast lingo that I must fill you in on. Ejector airtime is measured as negative G-force that is less than zero-G's. It is typically less sustainable but packs more of a punch. It gives off the impression to riders that they are coming out of their seat. Floater airtime is similar in that sense but is more sustainable and provides more of a weightless sensation (the force level of zero-G's) rather than the sensation of being thrown out of their seat.

There are numerous ride manufacturers that have models referred to as their "hyper coasters." I previously mentioned B&M and Arrow Dynamics, but companies by the name of "Morgan" (D.H Morgan Manufacturing – now defunct), as well as "Mack Rides" should be noted as well. Morgan hyper coasters are older and tend to have transitions that aren't as smooth. Nevertheless, these airtime-filled layouts still provide a solid ride experience. On the other hand, Mack Rides is a great manufacturer that we'll touch base with later. Long story short, their hyper coasters can provide smooth yet very intense ride experiences. They also may provide excellent ejector airtime.

B&M Inverted coasters: This is relatively self-explanatory, but inverted coasters are coasters in which riders sit below the track rather than above it. B&M have perfected their inverted model as many parks have them. Typically, inverted coasters have at least four inverts, including a vertical loop. The layouts for these inverts often also include a helix, and these tend to cause riders to pull major G's. When it comes to the inverted coaster, the B&M's are heavily favored. Another inverted model you may come across is the "Vekoma SLCs."

Vekoma Suspended Looping Coasters: Vekoma Suspended Looping Coasters hurt. I personally have heard nothing but bad things about these models. They are rough and *will* cause you to bash your head against the uncomfortable restraints. As for the layouts, they are all the same (although not terrible layouts).

Flying coasters: Yet another self-explanatory one, and yet another model B&M has also perfected. Riders get seated as if it were a normal inverted model, but before the ride starts, the ride vehicles flip to where they are in a superman position. Flying coasters offer riders unique sensations and allow for creativity in layout design. Pretzel loops are vertical loops in which riders dive downwards until they are head over heels and then on their backs. At the bottom, there is a great potential for pulled heavy G's. I've personally blacked out before on one of these elements. The pretzel formation of the loop is completed once you are propelled back up into your initial position.

This may seem like deja-vu; however, there is also a Vekoma alternative to this B&M coaster that isn't as good. Unfortunately, there are only a few left in existence. The first ever flying coaster was not built by B&M but rather by Vekoma, as these are referred to as the Vekoma Flying Dutchmans.

Shuttle coaster: Shuttle coasters do not make a complete circuit. This infers that (if riding a shuttle coaster), you will go backward. Statistically speaking, you will likely find yourself running into a Vekoma Boomerang model (Vekoma being the manufacturer). There are over 50 of these models dispersed across parks around the world. These models have a cobra roll as well as a vertical loop.

Tip 17: A cobra roll is an element that contains a half loop and then a perpendicular corkscrew followed by a complete vertical loop.

The Boomerang model brings you up the lift hill backward until it releases you, then you run through the course. Afterward, you head up the other lift hill right by the other one, and then it releases you backward, and you go through the layout backward. It's quite dizzying, and they can be rather rough sometimes since the manufacturer Vekoma (in their earlier models) had a bad reputation for not being the smoothest rides.

Giga coasters: Giga coasters are defined as rides that exceed 300 feet. Both B&M and the Swiss Manufacturer "Intamin" have a mean Giga coaster model. Intamin's *Millennium Force* was voted in the Golden Ticket Awards as the best steel roller coaster seven years in a row, only to be replaced by B&M's Fury 325, which has an excellent layout that rips through a course topping out at 95 mph.

Wooden coasters: Rides made of wood are basically their own category. "Woodies" can either be filled with gut-wrenching airtime hills in "out and back layouts" or can have "twister layouts," in which the layout is filled with twists, turns, and all sorts of laterals. GCI (Great Coasters International), an American-based company, creates the smoothest and highest quality wooden coasters. On the other hand, the "out and back layouts" are exactly what they sound like. These layouts tend to be airtime filled, in which the blueprint consists of back-to-back airtime hills, followed by a turnaround, and then more airtime hills that run alongside the previous airtime hills back to the station. These coasters are made with wood supports and wood tracks with a flat steel strip on top of the track.

Traditionally, this is what wooden roller coasters were confined to.

Tip 18: Son of Beast (now defunct since 2009) debuted at Kings Island in 2000. Here, a steel vertical loop was added to the layout, which technically made this the first inverting wooden roller coaster.

This was, technically, true; however, the loop was steel. It wasn't until 2013 when *Hades 360* at Mount Olympus added a 360-degree inverting roll manufactured by "The Gravity Group." A few years later, a company named "RMC" or "Rocky Mountain Construction" bombarded the scene with a new innovative wooden roller coaster topper track. These tracks allowed for layouts that could perform corkscrews, zero-G stalls, and other unheard-of types of inverting maneuvers on a wooden coaster. Fortunately, this wasn't the only innovation RMC would introduce to the coaster world.

Steel/Wooden Hybrid coasters: This category of coasters is only offered at the moment by RMC, as RMC developed the concept. Suppose your local park has an old and unpopular wooden roller coaster. Nobody waits in line to ride it because it's alarming to visitors that the fellow visitors who had just gotten off the ride tend to head straight to the nurse's office to get some ibuprofen. This is where RMC puts a dent in the big pharma business because people will no longer need ibuprofen. RMC turns these old, crusty, wooden roller coasters into one of the world's most thrilling, airtime-inducing, steel hybrid roller coasters. Using the already existing wooden supports, RMC designs a roller coaster with their steel "I-Box" track. These hybrids are favorites by pretty much all coaster enthusiasts, as these thrilling steel coasters (compared to their predecessor) will be taller, faster, more intense, more laterals, more airtime, more inversions... the whole enchilada. We'll discuss a few of these coasters throughout the book, so stay tuned.

Raptors: This is yet another model unique to the company RMC. These coasters are unique because they run on a single rail, as the riders ride in a single file line. This allows for tighter maneuvers, elements, inversions, and hills. Riders who have ridden these before report a very whippy experience in which they feel as if they are absolutely flying through the course.

The future of RMC: Considering this book is being written in the year 2022, I must mention the future of the company in case this book is being read in a later year. A few years ago, the coaster enthusiast community and amusement parks alike had learned of the new "T-Rex" track designed by RMC. T-rex track is a larger single rail track that will allow for even more impressive models than just the raptors. Will RMC manufacture larger-scale raptors with this track? Will they build inverting Giga coasters? We know that this track can be shaped to do incredible things; all that's left is to see what the future holds for the company.

Floorless/Sit-down roller coasters: Now that we've gone over RMC, it's time to give our friends over at B&M some attention again. They've missed us. One of the more common B&M models you'll find is their floorless models.

Tip 19: B&M roller coasters tend to have similar layouts to one another. The same vertical loops, corkscrews (sometimes interlocking corkscrews), and cobra rolls are found on nearly most B&M roller coasters that do, in fact, go upside down.

Likewise, the sit-down models are similar to the floorless, with the difference being obvious... your feet touch the ground on the sit-down model, whereas they dangle off the ground on the floorless model.

Obviously, the category of "floorless" and "sit-down" coasters is pretty loose. For this reason, I also find this to be an appropriate time to discuss Mack Rides and what they create (which aligns with this category). They too have a model known as "the Mega coaster," which are great rides with breathtaking inversions and whippy transitions and turns.

If you ever find yourself at a park staring at an old and janky looping coaster, chances are, it was built by Arrow Development and is an "Arrow Looping Coaster."

Arrow Dynamics is now defunct, but nevertheless, the company left a legacy of innovation. Arrow Development used to be *the* premier roller coaster manufacturer. They built the world's first inverting roller coaster.

Tip 20: "Corkscrew" opened at Knott's Berry Farm in 1975 as the world's first inverting roller coaster; the ride is considered a prototype. It now operates at Silverwood Theme Park in Idaho.

The ride features two back-to-back corkscrews. This paved the way for Arrow to build more of these looping coasters, many of which are still in operation despite being built in the 1970s–1990s. During the manufacturer's prime, their coasters were considered ground-breaking as they were setting records for the number of inversions on a roller coaster. Their looping coasters often came set with seven inversions, including loops, corkscrews, and even batwing elements (a heart-shaped element that is the inverse of a cobra roll – a half corkscrew which is followed up by a half-loop). From my experience, these rides tend to be a bit rough, and they may induce some headbanging.

Nevertheless, they aren't the worst coasters out there. I've ridden *Viper* at Six Flag Magic Mountain, and I actually enjoy the thrills of the ride. The loops are tight and rather intense because of how they are shaped. I also must mention that because these rides are a bit older, the transitions are not as smooth or enjoyable.

Strata coasters: Now, we're going to review some launched coasters. Strata coasters go over 400 feet, making them the tallest type of roller coaster. *Superman Escape from Krypton* at Six Flags Magic Mountain was the first to do this. This also was a shuttle coaster, as the ride consisted of a 100 mph launch, going up the spike, then down the spike, and into the station. At the time a very innovative ride for its sheer stats, but clearly not creative in the layout. *Kingda Ka (456 ft. tall – the tallest coaster in the world)* and *Top Thrill Dragster* are both world-renowned roller coasters that include launches well over 100 mph before heading up a spike and then down with a twisted drop plummeting to the ground. Once again, clearly, not a creative layout, but these steel giants' sheer size and speed make them quite extraordinary and exhilarating experiences. As impressive as these coasters are, you will not come across many strata coasters as not many of them exist around the globe.

Intamin and the hydraulic launch: The first predecessor to Kingda Ka and Top Thrill Dragster opened up at Knott's Berry Farm as a prototype by the name of *Xcelerator*.

Tip 21: Hydraulic launches use hydraulic fuel, and pressurized oil propels a ride vehicle forward or backward along the launch track.

Xcelerator may be a few hundred feet shorter in height, but it does not lack any intensity whatsoever. The success of Xcelerator paved the way for Intamin to create more of these models. In a sense, they are shorter versions of their strata coaster models to the extent that they have a top hat.

Tip 22: A "top hat" is an element on many launched coasters in which riders ascend at 90 degrees, twist (laterally) 90 degrees in which you'll experience airtime cresting over the hill (on some top hats), then another 90 degrees lateral twist that faces you back in the direction to which you came, and ending (in most instances) with 90 degrees drop.

Premier Rides Launched Coasters: Premier Rides is another ride manufacturer on which we haven't touched base. They were the first the use the **LIM (or Linear Induction Motors),** which led the way for the newer **LSM (Linear Synchronous Motors)** launch systems. For their launched coasters, both systems use magnetic pull to which electrical impulses are used to attract magnetic firm beneath the ride vehicle to propel it forward. Premier

Rides has a myriad of creative launched coaster models. Although their "Sky-Rockets" are often cloned at many parks, they include an "inline twist" in which riders are dangled upside down 150 feet in the air. Premier Rides manufactures all types of launched coasters, and they design innovative and exciting custom layouts. *Full Throttle* is a ground-breaking attraction with a 160-foot loop in which the top portion of the loop track is double-sided, meaning riders ride on both sides of the loop, riding over the loop at the end. Other than these, there are several other exciting coasters they've built, all of them whipping riders through countless inversions.

Gerstlauer Euro-Fighters: Euro-Fighters are cool looking attractions; they are quite the crowd pleasers. They start the ride experience with a 90-degree lift hill, followed by an even steeper beyond vertical drop. These intense little things typically aren't too tall, in many instances not even reaching 100 feet tall. They also are very compact and fit on a small blueprint. Despite this fact, they have no shortage of dizzying inversions (often loops, barrel rolls, cobra rolls, zero-G rolls, and even zero-G stalls).

Dive coasters: I was tempted to put "B&M Dive coasters," but there are, in fact, a few companies that manufacture dive coasters. B&M's Dive coasters are the most common and tend to be (as coaster enthusiasts call them) "one-trick ponies.

Tip 23: "One trick ponies" is an expression that describes a coaster that relies on one element to excite and "wow" its riders. Typically, coasters that are "one trick ponies" will have one element that enthusiasts will rave about, but the rest of the ride is considered forgettable and nothing to rave about.

For dive coasters, that one element is the first drop. Dive coasters are known to dangle riders over the ledge of the first drop. Once the train is released, riders plummet down a vertical drop.

Afterward, the rest of the layout depends on the park's budget for the coaster. Some dive coasters will go through a series of inversions such as vertical loops, Immelmann loops, and even zero-G rolls.

Tip 24: Immelmann loops start like a vertical loop, but halfway through the loop, the ride vehicle twists out of the loop and becomes right side up.

There are also dive coasters that are manufactured by Gerstlauer. Gerstlauer has a model that goes by the name of the "Infinity" model. We'll discuss the infinity model a bit more in just a moment. Some infinity models are dive coasters as well, they are pretty similar to the Euro-Fighter, but they dangle riders over the ledge of the first drop. I suppose this qualifies them to be dive coasters because other than this, there is no difference between these "infinity models" and the "Euro-Fighters" other than the size of the trains and riders they carry.

Gerstlauer Infinity coasters: These models are tough to describe because Gerstlauer can do so many things with this model. Unlike other models, there isn't necessarily a stereotypical layout for this model. Infinity coasters may have a launch or a vertical lift hill. The models they display on their website may have two inversions or 14 (you heard me right). In some instances, Euro-Fighters can be airtime focused. Infinity coasters have special features. They can come with a switch track, rotating platform, or even a reverse freefall in the layout (think of a spike in which riders head up the spike, don't make it all the way up, and head backward). Similar to the Euro-Fighters, they tend not to be the tallest coasters, but if there's anything you'll learn in this book, it's that the height doesn't necessarily go hand in hand with ride intensity.

Stand-up coasters: This is self-explanatory, but stand-up coasters are roller coasters in which riders... well, stand up. Yup, you heard me right. They stand up throughout the ride. B&M has manufactured the majority of stand-up coasters that exist, and they have similar layouts to their floorless coasters. One issue with most stand-coasters: they aren't comfortable. This complaint is predominantly expressed by men for obvious reasons. For this reason, parks have begun to convert their stand-up coasters into floorless ones.

4D roller coasters/free-spins: Remember the Arrow Development Company we discussed earlier? You might have been wondering *why* they are defunct. Although there were a few reasons why this manufacturer ended up becoming defunct, a pivotal reason was the construction of the world's first 4D roller coaster, *X2*. Unfortunately, the company misjudged the cost of building the ride by millions of dollars. We'll discuss X2 later in this book, as it's definitely a ride worth adding to your bucket list. With 4D coasters, riders sit on the side of the track. Throughout the ride experience, riders may flip upside down as their seats can rotate 360 degrees. In some instances, the flipping is controlled, and in other instances, the flipping isn't controlled. Instead, it is impacted by the weight and weight distribution of the ride vehicle. This is particularly the case with the "S&S free-spin" coasters, in which track is vertically stacked on top of each other with a beyond vertical drop that brings riders down a level at a time. S&S also built *Eejanaika; this* was essentially a taller, better, and smoother version of X2 that was constructed after Arrow Dynamics went bankrupt and was unable to manufacture this particular ride themselves.

Wing coasters: These are another model B&M Real Estate will primarily manufacture now, although Intamin has toyed with them. Just as you can tell from the name "wing" coaster, riders sit to the side of the track, two on each side. There have also been a few launched winged coasters. Something unique to winged coasters may be if they have a wing-over drop, in which the ride vehicles roll 180 degrees (inducing a 180 degrees switch in direction as well) and flip riders over before dropping. Near miss effects are also a factor of these rides, making them terrifying crowd pleasers.

Tip 25: Near miss effects are exactly what it sounds like. Particularly with winged coasters, the ride vehicles will race through a keyhole or a tight space in which riders feel as if they will hit or run into the keyhole or building they are passing through. These may also give the general public a terrifying picture. Obviously, safety requirements are made to which these near miss effects are no cause for safety concern.

Wild mouse coasters: These wacky-looking coasters are built to please families. You may recognize these coasters for their 180 degrees hairpin turns that make riders feel as if they are about to fly off the track (because the hairpin turns are not banked whatsoever). These coasters will also come with dips and dives, but nothing too crazy or intense for younger kids to handle.

Bobsled coasters: These tend to be rare. The track is basically a pipe in which riders sit in bobsleds. There are less than 10 in operation left. Amongst the ones open, Mack Rides and Intamin have built these, but in one special instance, the park itself built its own. Knoebles built their own wooden bobsled, which is named *Flying Turns*. Although uniquely enough, this is also the only operating wooden bobsled; the rest of the operating bobsleds are made of steel.

Suspended coasters: Back to Arrow Development (which many, quite frankly, will refer to as Arrow Dynamics), suspended coasters were quite the crowd-pleasers back in their "hey-day." Nowadays, they don't get the longest lines, but they do make for good family coasters. They are similar to inverted coasters in the manner that riders sit below the track. However, here is where the difference lies: there is no inversion; riders don't have their feet dangling, and the ride vehicles are connected with a swinging arm that can swing freely and pivot from side to side.

Spinning coasters: At first, spinning coasters were primarily family rides. When it comes to spinning coasters, they are essentially putting the Disneyland teacups on a roller coaster track. Boom, genius. Both Gerstlauer and Mack Rides have good spinning coaster models. Gerstlauer, specifically, make good family spinning roller coasters in which riders freely spin on an axis around a windy track with many banked turns and helixes.

On the other hand, *Mack Rides also* makes family-oriented spinning coasters but has also decided to cross boundaries and begin manufacturing *thrilling* spin coasters. Take *Time Traveler* at Silver Dollar City, for instance, which has two LSM launches, three inversions, and a 95-foot vertical drop. All while... yes, spinning.

Tip 26: I would suggest that if there is, in fact, a spinning coaster at the park you're visiting, be sure to consider riding it multiple times and in different rows and directions facing on the ride vehicles. What makes these such great attractions is that no two experiences are the same, so each new ride is a different experience.

Mine trains: Disney especially loves to build these in their parks. This is the case because mine trains are always family attractions. Mine trains (overwhelmingly) are either built into a man-made mountain, like *Thunder Mountain*, are indoors, or built using the terrain. They tend to be janky and windy but very organic and definitely not cookie-cutter. The ride vehicles will always depict mine train carts, and sometimes a front car (without riders) will depict a steam locomotive. *Toot toot*

Water coaster: I'll start by stating the obvious: these get you wet. I'd also say that water coasters, in terms of their layout, are one-trick ponies considering "the big drop" is what these rides are centered around. Other than that, all I can say is that I hope you decided to ride these on a hot day or else you'll be freezing.

Racing coaster: To state the obvious, if a roller coaster (which may land as another category on this list) races, then they are, in fact, a "racing coaster." Wooden coasters, steel hybrids, and premier rides launching coasters tend to be roller coasters that have layouts in which two ride vehicles race one another along their sets of track. In most instances, the layouts are designed for the sets of tracks to interact with one another. Either the coasters will have two separate tracks and therefore two separate rides, or it will be Mobius or a Mobius looping coaster. When a coaster has one of these layouts, this essentially means that the coaster is one long connected track with two sets of tracks that race one another.

Whew! That's a lot of information. As you can tell, there are numerous ways to categorize roller coasters. What you'll also notice is that there are roller coasters that may find themselves in more than one category. For instance: say there is a Dive coaster that is over the height of 200 feet. Because it is over 200 feet tall, it would also be deemed a hyper coaster. You've learned a giant hunk of the roller coaster enthusiast language here. Whenever you'd like, feel free to refer back to this guide. Now that we've covered roller coasters, we will review the other types of rides you'll come across.

Flat Rides

They may not be attached to roller coaster track or attract a three-hour wait, but they will still lift riders to impressive heights (often higher than roller coasters), invert guests upside down, pull negative and positive G's, as well induce plenty of screams. Here is an overview of the various types of flat rides you will encounter when visiting the parks.

Drop Towers

These are the tallest flat rides you'll come across. In some instances, they will also be the tallest attraction a park has to offer to its guests. Drop towers are (obviously) towers that bring guests up to the top and then drop them (I bet you found *that* surprising). There is some variation, however, between some drop towers. For instance, some (manufactured by S&S) will actually launch riders up the tower before they propel back down. Other drop towers (manufactured by Intamin) will tilt riders towards to ground before releasing the gondola. Parks may also decide to attach a drop tower to a roller coaster as the coaster's supports may also provide support for a drop tower. Examples of this would come in the form of *Zumanjaro Drop of Doom* which is attached to *Kingda Ka*, or *Lex Luther Drop of Doom* which is attached to *Superman Escape from Krypton.*

Interestingly enough, both drop towers here belong to Six Flags parks.

Tip 27: *If you ever get the chance to ride* Lex Luther Drop of Doom *at Six Flags Magic Mountain, don't be surprised if you feel the entire structure shaking while headed up to the top of the tower.*

The tower sways when Superman's vehicles race up the tower, and *you will* feel that swaying when riding this drop tower. Don't worry; you'll only be about 400 feet up in the air, so there's nothing to worry about.

Pendulum Swings

I love these things, but I am aware of the fact that many don't because they induce nausea. And nausea induces throwing up, which may ruin your day at the park.

Tip 28: Don't ride a pendulum swing if you think you're running the risk of throwing up OR if you've eaten lunch or dinner within the last half-hour.

So, by all means, Pendulum swings are simple; you rock back and forth and swing in circles. The seating arrangements may differ as riders either sit on a giant frisbee and face outwards (these are the giant frisbees/pendulum swings) that may go over 100 feet in the air. These are manufactured by a company named "Zamperla," as numerous parks are adding these to their lineup of flat rides.

Tip 29: Parks find it important to diversify the types of thrill rides they offer to their guests, which is why having a solid flat ride lineup is also important.

Smaller-scale pendulum rides tend to have riders facing inwards, as there are four gondolas with a certain amount of riders in each gondola. Either way, you swing up and down and all around. A few models also go in loops and flip riders upside down, although you won't come across these models very frequently.

Screamin Swings

These are even more simple than pendulum swings. These don't even spin riders. It's essentially a large-scale pneumatic powered swing that (once again) S&S manufactures. There's a frame, and then the one or two arms holding the riders in which they swing back and forth. Like I said, pretty simple.

Sky Screamers/Swings

If the park's drop tower isn't quite the tallest attraction in the park, there is also a chance that the sky screamer is. Hopefully, you are aware of or have likely seen the swing rides in which you take your seat on the chair attached to a chain in which you get lifted up and go around in circles. These are your classic swing rides. Sky screamers take this concept and make the structure hundreds of feet tall and much, much faster. Still, you are held up with chains. But don't worry, they're safe rides. I promise.

Ferris Wheels

These are classic. And likely, unless you've been living under a rock for your entire life, you know what these are. You take your seat, go up as the wheel turns, and then you go down and end up where you started once the wheel has made its full rotation.

Carousel

Yes, these are technically flat rides... next!

Flying Scooters

These are pretty cool rides; they are typically referred to as "Flyers." The ride vehicles, which are obviously suspended and connected to the center support, swing around in circles. These attractions started making the rounds (no pun intended) in the 1930s, but then a manufacturer named "Larson International" brought back the attraction to which many parks installed them. I personally find these cool because when the ride vehicles spin, they spin, turning outwards. The riders can control how the vehicle turns with a rudder.

Enterprises

These come set with 20 gondolas. There is a spinning wheel sitting on its side that swings the gondolas (each attached going around the side of the circle), to which the wheel eventually lifts off the ground and turns as it lifts until the wheel becomes turned vertical. Finally, once the arm that lifts the wheel is at its highest point, the riders are essentially going upside around in loops. Eventually, the ride returns to how it started.

Top Spins

On top spins, two arms (which turn with motors) hold up a giant gondola/platform that may even hold up to 77 passengers (if, in fact, it's a Giant Top Spin). Top Spins are full of swinging loops, being held upside for longer durations of time, and all sorts of logic-defying sensations. The giant arms turn, which spins the platform, which can be held with brakes, which is why there are instances when riders are held upside down; the motors interact with the brakes, which makes the gondola rotate and complete all the various maneuvers. Of the flat rides we've gone through, these are the most difficult to describe when considering the mechanisms of the attraction and how it works.

Gravitron

If I'm being honest, I hate these things. You may find these at some parks, but you will mainly find these at your local carnival. These things spin you really fast, and the centripetal force sticks riders to the wall. Some skilled riders are even able to do flips and all sorts of tricks while riding, although I'd imagine snapping my neck if I made the same attempts.

Tip 30: *Don't ride these attractions too frequently in a short period of time, or you'll throw up due to intense nausea like I did when I was 13.*

Slingshot

These catapult riders into the sky as they get slingshot up in a capsule while simultaneously pulling heavy G's and sensations of weightlessness. The capsules also flip like there's no tomorrow. You may have come across YouTube compilation videos of riders passing out on these things because they are, in fact, very intense rides. The downside to these is that amusement parks tend to make these "upcharge" attractions.

Tip 31: Upcharge attractions are attractions in which the park charges its guests an extra fee to ride. If you plan on riding a slingshot on your next visit to the park, be sure to do your research on the park's website to check how much they charge to ride.

Air Races

These are newer to the world of flat rides. Basically, riders get in their ride vehicles and spin around in circles. Simultaneously, you're swinging left to right and right to left until, eventually, you're doing flips. One arm is holding the gondola, while there's an arm attached to that arm that holds the gondola and does the loops and swinging. The gondolas look like planes because these air races are supposed to emulate an acrobatic flight.

Bumper cars

These are good times, especially when you have family or friends competing with you to try to hit one another. I don't really need to go into detail about how these work or what they do. But for those who *have* been living under a rock, or maybe live in Kansas, you basically drive a little vehicle around and try to bump other cars. Rubber bumpers surround the vehicles, so don't worry; no airbags will go off, nor will your vehicle be totaled. Woohoo... fun!

These are most of the notable flat rides you may encounter during your next visit to the park. For any flat ride that I didn't go over or review, just keep this in mind:

All flat rides

- Either spin, swing, or flip in some way (unless it's a drop tower)
- Will induce nausea if not ridden in moderation
- Are not roller coasters

The Larson Super loop

Super loops are flat rides as well, but Six Flags would beg to differ for marketing purposes. Here's the deal: a super loop is that ride you'll come across at the carnival in which it's just a giant loop. The ride is quite simple; you get into the train and go through the only atmosphere possible with the super loop: a loop. In recent years, Six Flags (the chin) would open and add a number of these to some of their parks, marketing them as a "roller coaster."

Tips 32: They are not considered roller coasters by coaster enthusiasts. Here's why: either the rides are tire driven, or the vehicles are attached to a conveyer belt that is locked within the track (depending on the manufacturer).

Nevertheless, these are advertised as roller coasters, but I, as well as other coaster enthusiasts, would again beg to differ. This is why I've decided to mention them after the flat rides section of the book rather than the roller coaster one.

Water Rides

splashes

This will likely be the shortest section of this chapter because there are only a few types of water rides that you may come across at an amusement park. These have the primary intention of getting riders wet and cooling them off on a hot summer day. In that instance, the line for the log flume or rapids ride may even compete with the steel titan roller coasters of the park because of how desperate guests are for a cool-off.

Log flumes

Log flumes are classic; in many cases, they don't require riders to put on a seat belt or restraint. Some log flumes are quite simple: you make a few mundane turns, go up a lift hill, go down a drop, get soaking wet, do a few more turns, and before you know it, someone else is sitting in the same water that just soaked your pants. In other instances, parks will theme their log flumes elaborately and add dark ride elements like animatronics, a storyline, and music/audio. They'll also have more drops and a longer layout in these instances.

Rapids

Get yourself into a group of five other friends with these, or at the very least,

Tip 33: Get to know the people you're riding with on these. You are destined to laugh and scream together over something as simple as getting wet.

Once you board the circular ride vehicles, you prepare yourself for the currents, waterfalls, spins, and drops. Most of you know how these ride experiences differ from others. Typically, there are one or two riders who get more soaked from the rest and are subject to laughter and jokes once the attraction comes to an end.

We also touched on "water coasters" earlier in the book. Feel free to flip back to the section in this chapter about roller coasters to refresh yourself. Other than that, if you wish to get wet and cool off in the summer heat, I'd recommend going to the water park that may or may not be located right by the amusement park you were originally going to go to.

Dark Rides

These tend to be the bread and butter of theme parks. These allow for the most immersive experiences that parks have to offer. In this section, we'll discuss the various types of dark rides and how they differ from one another.

Motion-based simulators

If you have been to Universal Studios, you are familiar with these. There seemed to be a point in time when the Universal near my house (Hollywood) had only two types of attractions. Their tram (which we discussed earlier) and motion-based simulator rides. The initial concept of a motion-based simulator was simple. There's a screen presenting a film in which the film is synchronized with the vehicle and the vehicle's motion. An easy example most of us are familiar with is *Star Tours* at Disneyland. This ride is very simple yet excellent. With these types of motion-based simulators, the size of the ride capsule varies with the capacity that it holds. The type of ride capsule or vehicle may also vary. Across the way from

Disneyland is Disney's California Adventure, which is host to *Soarin' over California*. It would also be a motion-based simulator in which riders sit and ride a glider with their feet dangling. You aren't enclosed in a capsule but rather open and free while facing a much larger screen. No 3D is needed here. Sometimes these motion-based simulators will have many capsules and ride vehicles apart from each other, all interacting with the same large theatre-sized (even sometimes larger) screen.

Since then, innovation within this category of theme park attraction has vastly accelerated. Later on, screen-based dark rides that weren't necessarily motion-based simulators in the traditional sense began to surface. *The Amazing Adventures of Spider-Man* opened in 1999, and this is a ride that many consider setting the bar for screen-based dark rides still. This now leads me to share about EMVs.

Tip 34: EMVs, or Enhanced Motion Vehicles, are at the center of this innovation that I speak of. We'll obviously discuss other types of dark rides later in this section of the book, and Enhanced Motion Vehicles are a game changer for many of these other types of dark rides.

These ride vehicles were initially designed for *Indiana Jones Adventure: Temple of the Forbidden Eye*. I won't confuse you with the intricate technology and functions of how these work, but I will attempt to give a brief overview of what these things can do. EMVs give rides a more realistic sensation, in which the motion is also immersive because of how well these vehicles are able to give off the movements of swaying, shaking, rolling, pitching, surging, and heaving. The vehicles themselves have a thrust plane and rotational axis, which allows for the various motions to be possible. What Universal was able to do with *The Amazing Adventures of Spider-Man* was incorporate these types of ride vehicles and combine them with the screen-motion-based ride experience. The EMVs sit on a track that brings riders through a set of screens that have different scenes. The ride does use 3D technology and also utilizes special effects like fog, fire, lights, heat, and even spraying water. This all together gives riders quite an impressive and immersive experience. Following suit rides like *Transformers: The Ride* has done the same while also using both animatronics and screens.

This is where we find ourselves in some gray areas. For example, many dark rides now incorporate both motion and screens as a part of the experience but also utilize other dark ride elements that you obviously wouldn't find in screen-based motion simulators. So do we discuss these types of rides in this category? Naw..., let's start a new category.

Motion-based dark rides

This is the best I could do for starting a new category. Notice the difference: "Motion-based simulators" and "Motion-based dark rides." Once a ride not only incorporates various other dark ride elements other than just the screens *and* sits on a track, I would no longer want to just limit it to the label of being a *simulator*. I will be honest when I say the difference between the two categories will put us in some gray areas with identifying certain attractions, even with The Amazing Adventures of Spider-Man.

Nevertheless, here we are. First, let's discuss motion-based dark rides. As I've mentioned, there are most certainly screens often involved with this specific category of a dark ride. This, along with animatronics, on-ride audio, special effects, and a storyline that puts riders right in the middle of the story are the elements that make up these rides. EMVs, being versatile, are able to motion-simulate to screens as well, simulate a jeep ride with the engine shaking (like Indiana Jones, which we mentioned earlier), and everything in between. So to sum it up, this category of dark rides (in most cases) combines the elements of going through a practical set, animatronics, and screen-based motion simulators. In a few other cases, dark rides will still utilize EMVs (like, once again, Indian Jones) but won't have screen-based features.

In recent years, innovation has been taken to a whole new level. Trackless dark rides with all these various elements are also taking the industry by storm.

Tip 35: Trackless dark rides advance how immersive a ride experience is. Think about it; a track is a constant reminder that you are on a ride. While amid an action-filled story, you look out in front of your ride vehicle and see that it's all a part of the plan. I am not in this dangerous situation because of the storyline, but rather because the vehicle has followed the track to this point. But when there is no track, this now is no longer an issue.

With trackless dark rides, the vehicles and how they move are automated. With the new *Star Wars: Rise of the Resistance* ride opened up at various Disney parks, I find myself concerned that we've reached the peak of innovation when it comes to this type of dark ride. The escape pods riders ride may not be EMV vehicles, but they don't *need* to be. We've now reached the point where we can have trackless vehicles. These vehicles can give any sensation of movement that can be simulated on screens or rides through a series of ultrarealistic animatronics. In addition, parks have all possible special effects at their disposal to give the most immersive and incredible ride experience possible. Impressive stuff, eh?

Nevertheless, I'd still categorize these as motion-based dark rides because of the immersive features that the EMVs provide and the fact that the ride vehicles aren't necessarily in tandem either. So what does "tandem" mean in this instance? Well, we must cover the category of "classic dark rides."

Classic dark rides

When I think of classic dark rides (I grew up going to Disneyland, yes, I know I am referencing the park a lot throughout this book), I think of the *Haunted Mansion.* You really don't get any more classic or basic of a dark ride than this. All the ride vehicles move in tandem and are sitting on a continuous moving strip. You get on, go through a series of sets, animatronics, and scenes, and get off. It's a neat ride experience and is, in its essence, a classic. The same could go for *It's a Small World* or *Pirates of the Caribbean.* These both are classic dark rides, except your mode of transportation is water. What more is there to say about classic dark rides? There is always a storyline, and you slowly move through the various scenes with a series of animatronics, special effects, and on-ride audio that is either coming from the vehicle or the sets themselves.

Interactive/Shooter dark rides

By the title of this category, it is quite apparent what stands out about these. In most instances, shooter/interactive dark rides incorporate 3D or 4D screens. In other cases, you'll find yourself on a classic dark ride that just so happens to have guns in which you're shooting for targets that are dispersed throughout the various sets. These tend to be fun if you are a competitive person who likes to obtain bragging rights. These rides also have a "re-rideability" factor.

Tip 36: A "re-rideability" factor is when a ride tends to motivate guests to get back on and ride again. Obviously, many associate a re-rideability factor with roller coasters, but ALL types of rides may have a re-rideability factor if they are in and of themselves excellent rides... unless they are interactive or shooter dark rides. An interactive or shooter dark ride will usually have a re-rideability factor because people love to compete against one another over and over again.

If you're a guy who happens to have a girlfriend (and you're a sore loser), and your girlfriend takes you down and scores higher than you, your fragile male ego will wish to ride again in an attempt to beat her so you can prove your lie of an excuse that "you were letting her win," was actually true. These tend to be great attractions the whole family can enjoy for these reasons.

Diversity in elements, vehicles, and category

This section of the book has been a bit tricky even for me to categorize, articulate, and inform with, simply because dark rides aren't as easily distinguishable from one another as roller coasters may be. You may, for instance, hear the term "dark ride elements" when someone is talking about a ride that *isn't* a dark ride.

Tip 37: "Dark ride elements" is a term often used by roller coaster enthusiasts when a ride (typically a roller coaster, but it may also be a water ride) has elements and features typical of a dark ride. Dark ride elements are storytelling elements in which animatronics, sets, and scenes are used on a ride that is either not a dark ride or is a hybrid between a dark ride and a roller coaster (which is common). For example, splash Mountain combines both a dark ride and a log flume but is primarily referred to as an impressive, classic log flume.

When discussing motion-based dark rides, I also made the point that there is a gray area with how we categorize specific rides on a ride-to-ride basis. Some ride vehicles are pods that fit 12 riders; others may have riders sit in a large theatre. Some dark rides are known for their impressive new-age animatronics. Still, some are roasted for having outdated animatronics in which riders are hopefully riding for the sake of a classic rather than an immersive experience.

Either way, this wraps up our overview of dark rides.

Chapter Review

- Not all rides are the same; we can divide them into basic categories: roller coasters, flat rides, water rides, and dark rides. Each category has its own subcategories as not all roller coasters are the same, nor are all dark rides the same.

- Roller coasters strive to thrill riders with intense forces or senses of weightlessness or airtime. They may invert riders, throw riders into twists and turns, laterals, or eject their butt off the seat over hills. Ride vehicles can sit or dangle riders below, above, or to the sides of the track. These are typically the main draw to most parks.
- Flat rides are typically the ones that will spin riders around, bring them up a tower and drop them, or flip guests uncontrollably while simultaneously sending them home nauseous (depending on their tolerance levels).
- Water rides have the intent of getting riders wet; why else would they be water rides? You may sit in a log, or you may sit around in a circle facing other riders on a rapids ride.
- Dark rides incorporate screens, animatronics, special effects, and at the center... a storyline that you have likely found yourself caught in the middle of. These are the bread and butter of theme parks in many instances. They may also be interactive in which riders compete against one another.

Chapter 3: How Expert's Best Amusement Parks Ranked 101 – 1

This list will be rather difficult and is obviously very subjective. Everybody has different tastes in which type of experience they desire. For example, a parent of two young children might appreciate a LEGOLAND park over a Six Flags park, even though most see the Six Flags park as the better park for the thrills that the park offers. Even people within a similar age demographic will disagree about what's key when deciding which park is superior. Some prefer immersive theming and beautiful landscaping, and others prefer the concrete jungle thrill park. So if I'm being honest, nobody (especially coaster enthusiasts) will agree with another's list.

So here are the criteria for this list:

- Roller coasters: Does the park have a well-rounded collection of roller coasters? Thrill and family? How is their "one-two punch?"

Tip 38: A "one-two punch" is similar to how people would look at a pitching rotation in baseball. The one-two punch is the top two rides at a park, and a good one-two punch will lead the lineup of coasters that a park has to offer.

- How is the park's collection of thrill flats, water rides, and family flats? Do they have an observation tower? What kind of lineup of rides do they have other than the selection of roller coasters?
- How is the food? Very important.
- How is the park's cleanliness? Did the park consider landscaping that comes set with
- plants, trees, and charm?

- Is the park well-themed? Or is it more of an "amusement park?" Very few parks can master theming and thrills; typically, parks choose one or the other. But parks that can do both will probably get bonus points.
- Does the park target a specific demographic, or is it a park that kids, teenagers, and parents can all enjoy alike? Bonus points to the park that can excite all age groups. This typically will depend on how well-rounded the line-up of rides are, in which they have something to offer for everyone.
- I will *not* be considering how expensive the park is as a part of the criteria. This is because pricier parks tend to be (not always, but usually) better quality, and vis-versa. Also, this is difficult to measure, considering that I personally have not attended every park on this list. In my fair opinion, the price of the park should not impact how great of a destination the park itself is.
- Is there anything that stands out about the park? Something unique that it's known for. Sometimes one world-class puts a park on the map and will ultimately lead to it being on this list.
- I also will consider animals. That's you, Sea World!
- Keep in mind that I want this list to be practical as well. I wanted to include parks from all over the world so whoever reads this will be able to identify a park within reach.

Obviously, most parks don't meet all of these criteria well. Most specialize in a few of these, but obviously, parks that can do all these things well will thrive on the list. Here is how the list follows:

- 101 – 50 will be a list to round out the top 101 parks. These parks are in no particular order. Number 94 may very well be just as good as a park as number 56. What each of these parks *does* share in common is that they are each top 101 amusement parks in our eyes. I will also be sure to include some minor details or facts regarding each park, including the park's location and specialty.
- 49 – 11 will be ranked in order. I will also be sure to give some more insight into why each of these parks is placed on the list where they are. Parks in this tier truly are world-

class, each of which has a standout attraction or feature that makes it a top tourist or roller coaster enthusiast destination.

- 10 -1 This is where things get controversial. Nobody can argue that each of these top ten parks is the cream of the crop, but nobody will agree on how they should be ranked. Nevertheless, I will be sure to go well in depth as to why each of these ten parks is one of the top ten amusement parks in the world.

So without further ado, here is HowExpert Guide's Top 101 Amusement Parks to visit:

How Expert's Top 101 Amusement Parks to Visit

Parks Ranked - 101 – 51

- **101. Lake Compounce**

Let's start this list with America's first theme park. Lake Compounce is rather quaint and located in Bristol and Southington, Connecticut. *Boulder Dash* is their headline attraction, a wooden terrain coaster in which riders fly through the hills and get excellent airtime.

Tip 39: Terrain coasters utilize the natural terrain in their layouts, which ensures a unique ride experience with plenty of character. Hills, valleys, and canyons make for the best opportunities in this instance.

- **100. Happy Valley Shanghai**

This park (obviously located in Shanghai) is a top destination for thrill seekers who live on China's central coast. They are home to *Diving Coaster*, which is by far the most creative name I've ever heard for a dive coaster!

- ## 99. Imagicaa

Although Essell World claims to be the largest amusement park in India, after further research, I can say with certainty that the top thrill seeker's destination in India is, in fact, Imagicaa. The park is located in Khopoli, India, and is by far the prettiest and most to-scale theme park that India has to offer. They even have a B&M floorless coaster.

- ## 98. Greenland

Greenland is a park in Arao, Kumamoto, Japan. The park is solid and has that Japanese amusement park charm to it, despite being a bit of a weird park with lots of random theming. They do house ten roller coasters, though, and I'd say it is worth a visit if you happen to be in the area.

- ## 97. Kentucky Kingdom

At one point, this park was shut down. Six Flags purchased it and revived it, adding both *Lightning Run* (a Chance Rides Hyper GTX model) as well as *Storm Chaser,* an RMC hybrid of the former *Twisted Twins* roller coaster. The park is located in Louisville, Kentucky.

- ## 96. SeaWorld San Antonio

Each of the three SeaWorld parks in the United States will find themselves on this list. The reason is that the future of each of these parks is bright for the thrill coaster category, as the chain invests heavily in this department. Obviously, the park has a collection of sea animals, but it also has its B&M invert as well as its Morgan hyper coaster, *Steel Eel.*

- ## 95. Six Flags Over Georgia

Goliath is a B&M hyper coaster regarded as one of the best. They, too, have opened up their revitalized RMC steel hybrid coaster and rounded out their top three with their Gerstlauer Euro-Fighter, or Batman clone (whichever you see as better). With Six Flags parks, you'll notice that I will usually only discuss the roller coasters and thrill rides selection, which is for a reason with these parks.

- ## 94. Beto Carrero World

This is Brazil's signature amusement park, which is why I decided to give it a place on this list. Its location is in Santa Catarina, Brazil, which gives it enough of a reason for me to include it. Unfortunately, the park's main thrill coasters are both older Vekoma models, but the park itself is full of color and beautiful trees. Their selection of family attractions is also pretty good, and they do attempt to give the park some decent theming as well.

- ## 93. Futuroscope

Now, *this* is something very different on the list. Not only does this French theme park have a very cool name, but it also has the unique quality of giving visitors a learning experience of multimedia audio-visual cinematic methods and techniques. The whole park is based on these technological effects and is home to (as you'd imagine) quite a few screen-based motion dark rides as well as an Intamin multi-launched spinning coaster. The theming with each of their attractions is obviously as excellent as you'd imagine as well.

- ## 92. Chimelong Ocean Kingdom

This park, located in Zhuhai, China, is on the newer side and is an incredible ocean-themed park with incredible underwater dome-shaped aquariums, ones that even blow SeaWorld out of the water (no pun intended), as they have record-sized aquariums. The rides are incredibly themed, and the park is even home to a B&M winged coaster named *Parrot Coaster*. The park is elaborately themed and is quite beautiful as well. I was really tempted to put this park in the top 50, but they were just slightly lacking in the rides department.

- ### 91. Paulton's Park

I had to shout this place out; they are home to Peppa Pig World. Located in Hampshire, England, this is an amazing family destination, specifically for the younger kids. The park is host to over 70 rides and attractions, but nothing to shout about. Peppa Pig World is what makes this a top 101 park, but if I were to have each of these parks in order, it would probably have been #101.

- ### 90. Universal Studios Beijing

Here is our first Universal Studios park, but actually the newest park on this entire list. Here, the park is host to its own *Wizarding World of Harry Potter* as well as its own *Jurassic World Adventure* water ride. Considering it just opened recently, there is plenty of room for expansion as the park looks to catch up to the other Universal parks.

- ### 89. World Joyland

Very rarely will I decide to put a park on this list primarily because of just one ride, but this park is an exception. The park is in Changzhou, China, and is home to quite possibly one of, if not *the*, best flying coaster in the world that goes by the name *Sky Scrapper*. Watch a POV of this ride on YouTube, trust me.

Tip 40: A "POV" or a "point of view" is a video in which you get a rider's point of view of riding the ride. A camera is mounted to the front of the train, or a rider is physically filming the attraction while riding.

- ### 88. Nasu Highland Park

Located in Nasu, Japan, this is yet another park that embodies that classic yet odd Japanese amusement park charm. The main attraction here is a weird roller coaster named *Big Boom,* which gets praised for its first drop and vertical loop.

- **87. Everland**

Here's a shoutout to South Korea's largest theme park, an absolutely stunning destination that is also home to Asia's best and most intense wooden coaster, *T Express.* This should be an enthusiast's top destination if they ever get the chance to visit South Korea.

- **86. Six Flags Discovery Kingdom**

This Northern California park is home to a solid lineup of coasters, including both a B&M floorless coaster and an RMC hybrid. They are also host to penguins, alligators, giraffes, and other wildlife creatures, which makes this Six Flags park, in particular, unique.

- **85. BonBon Land**

I feel that even most roller coaster enthusiasts aren't aware of this Danish theme park in South New Zealand. I had to mention it because the park brands itself as "Denmark's funniest amusement park," which comes set with a myriad of attractions for the kids but also a Euro-Fighter. The park is filled with theming that aims to make people laugh but at the cost of having a reputation of being a weird and quirky park that isn't for everyone, especially if dry humor is more of your thing.

- **84. Asterix Park**

This park, located in France, is based on the comic book series "Asterix." I mention this because Asterix Park is elaborately themed with its architecture, statues, landscaping, and everything in between. They also have a B&M invert.

Tip 41: Something you'll notice is that European parks tend to be superior when it comes to theming.

- **83. Djurs Sommerland**

Djurs Sommerland deems itself to be "Scandinavia's biggest summerland." The park's standout attractions are an Intamin sit-down coaster and a pirate-themed water coaster that happens to be the largest water coaster in Northern Europe. In 2022 they are opening up "Dinosaurland," which is their newly themed area with 25 animatronic Dinosaurs.

- **82. La Ronde**

Quite honestly, this park would probably be closer to #101 if we were to rank each and every park on this list. Nevertheless, this park has value because it still has a decent collection of thrill rides, including *Goliath,* which is a B&M "hyper coaster" model, but it doesn't quite reach 200ft. ." The park also happens to have an above-average collection of thrilling flat rides as well.

Tip 42: After attending multiple Six Flags parks, you'll notice that Six Flags parks can't help but name their rides "Goliath

- **81. Ocean Park**

Ocean Park claims to be "Hong Kong's Best Theme Park." And maybe, just maybe, it is. Either way, I see this park as sort of the Hong Kong's version of Sea World. They seem to have an exciting collection of animals, from pandas to sharks and even Arctic foxes. They also have some thrilling flat rides and a B&M floorless coaster.

- **80. Gardaland**

It's becoming a reoccurring thing to mention that parks are claiming to be "the best in their respected country," and Gardaland is no different. They claim to be "Italy's number 1 amusement resort." I do consider this park to be well-rounded with both family and thrill attractions. They have both a B&M dive and winged coaster as a solid one-two punch, as well a Vekoma SLC that should be shut down and replaced with a B&M invert.

- **79. Parque Warner Madrid**

Located in Madrid, Spain, this park comes set with shows, restaurants, thrill rides, family attractions, and everything in between. I'd consider this a decently well-rounded park with movie-themed lands and attractions, as well as a few solid B&M roller coasters. They also have an inverted boomerang named *Stunt Fall*, which I find to be a very fitting name for the ride model.

- **78. Worlds of Fun**

Aside from being the largest amusement park in the U.S. Midwest and the very wholesome name of the park, Worlds of Fun has an excellent family atmosphere in which it has themed areas of different parts of the world, hence the name "Worlds" of Fun. In terms of the rides lineup, there is a decent mix of family and thrill flats, as well as a decent roller coaster lineup that includes a Morgan Hyper coaster, *Mamba,* and a B&M inverted coaster named *Patriot*. I assume *Patriot* is in the USA-themed part of the park.

- **77. Nickelodeon Universal at Mall of America**

This is the first of two Nickelodeon Universe parks. This one is at the famous Mall of America in Bloomington, Minnesota. The park is themed to the classic Nickelodeon shows and characters, most notably SpongeBob, Jimmy Neutron, and The Fairly Odd Parents, to name a few. *SpongeBob SquarePants Rock Bottom Plunge* is their headliner attraction, which is a Gerstlauer Euro-Fighter. They also have an excellent collection of family thrill rides and attractions. The indoor park is full of vibrant theming and color.

From what I've heard, it also has a better atmosphere than the other Nickelodeon Universe.

- ## 76. Nickelodeon Universe at America Dream

American Dream Mall is located in East Rutherford, New Jersey, and is home to (as more consider it to be) an even better lineup of thrill coasters and flat rides *TMNT Shell Raiser* is their headlining attraction that happens to have the world's steepest drop. They also have a smaller scale Intamin launched coaster and an excellent family coaster named *Nickelodeon Slime Streak*. Like the other Nickelodeon Universe, the park is a melting pot of Nickelodeon theming of all the classic Nickelodeon shows and characters.

- ## 75. Mt. Olympus

If I'm being honest, I've heard quite the mixed reactions to this park. Nevertheless, they

boast a few impressive wooden coasters, including *Hades 360,* which is widely considered one of the best and most intense wooden roller coasters out there. Other than this, there isn't much to say about this park. The theming isn't anything too special, but at least

Tip 43: (from what I've seen) the park is very affordable and gives good deals on ticket and hotel prices! In fact, they have $25.00 tickets on their website at the moment this book is being written.

- ## 74. Happy Valley Shenzhen

Here's another Happy Valley park that had to be included on the list. Their top attraction is... you guessed it... a roller coaster. *Bullet Coaster,* which is an S&S air-compression launched coaster that happens to launch riders at 83 mph and drop them over 200 feet. Unfortunately, they do not have a strong one-two punch, as their next largest ride is a Vekoma SLC. Nevertheless, I'd consider this 86-acre park to host one of China's better roller coaster collections. The park also has nine themed areas, a few of these being "Cartoon City" and "Gold Mine Town."

- ## 73. Valleyfair

Valleyfair, located in Shakopee, Minnesota, is home to a celebratory atmosphere with a decent collection of thrill coasters and family rides. Their top three include a Morgan Hyper coaster, *Wild Thing,* an Intamin inverted launched shuttle coaster, *Steel Venom,* and a GCI Woodie, *Renegade.*

Tip 44: It is, in fact, appropriate to call a wooden coaster a "Woodie." This way, you're guaranteed to sound like a coaster enthusiast.

- ## 72. LEGOLAND, California & LEGOLAND, Florida

These parks are *made* for younger children, but quite honestly, I myself would be excited to attend this park just for the Lego showcases they have and the marvelous sculptures and cities they build and invite guests to discover. These theme parks immerse guests in wonderlands of Lego-themed areas and have no shortage of family rides, attractions, and shows.

- ## 71. Dorney Park

I'd like to include Dorney Park, Valleyfair, as well as Worlds of Fun as our little group of mid-tier Cedar Fair parks. One thing they all have in common: a Morgan Hyper coaster; Dorney's is named *Steel Force.* Dorney has the better of the three thrill lineups, as they have an excellent B&M Floorless coaster, as well as an even more excellent B&M Invert, *Talon.* With an overall solid collection of thrill rides and even some family rides, Dorney is worth a good visit.

Tip 45: Their B&M Invert, named Hydra, has a unique element known as the "JoJo roll. This element is essentially a heartline roll before the lift hill, which slowly flips riders upside before the ride has even really gotten going.

- ## 70. Tokyo Dome City

Okay, maybe Tokyo Dome City doesn't quite have a full collection of rides for you to want to spend the *whole* day there. Still, they do have *Thunder Dolphin,* this super unique and rather tall Intamin hyper coaster that utilizes tall buildings in the heart of Tokyo with its layout. It's freaking awesome. The park also has a great-looking Ferris wheel. So maybe they only have a few rides, but it's worth a visit. The area is full of tourist attractions considering this little park is smack dab right in the heart of Tokyo.

- ## 69. Warner Bros Movie World

Finally, some representation for you Australian citizens. How's it going, mate? This park has a similar make-up to its sister Warner Bros parks as well as the Universal parks. What makes this the better Warner Bros park is the one-two-three punch of *DC Rivals Hypercoaster* and Intamin hyper coaster with an intense layout that is sure to give some ejector airtime as well as cause you to gray out on an empty stomach. *Also, Superman Escape*, an Intamin launched coaster with a brilliant layout, as well as *Green Lantern Coaster*, an "El Loco" model that defies all reason and logic (just watch a POV of it).

Tip 46: If you know before riding a coaster that it will pull heavy G's and be very intense, be sure not to ride it on an empty stomach, or else you will increase your chance of blacking out or losing your vision in the G's inducing portions of the ride.

- ## 68. Walibi Belgium

Here's some representation for Wavre, Belgium. Their new coaster, *Kondaa,* is an Intamin mega coaster that basically combines a hyper coaster and a sit-down inverting coaster. They also have an okay collection of supporting coasters (other than the Vekoma SLC) but a rather impressive collection of family-oriented flats and coasters. The park also looks to be well landscaped with lakes and trees. All in all, this park is legit and worth checking out if you're in the area.

- ### 67. Happy Valley Beijing

This is the other Happy Valley that we'll touch base on with this list. Happy Valley Beijing has well executed theming of the Greek and Mayan cultures. They have a B&M flyer, *Crystal Wing,* S&S compressed air launch coaster, *Extreme Rusher,* and a pretty rad Mine Train coaster, *Jungle Racing.* The park seems to be well-rounded for families as well.

- ### 66. Movie Park Germany

Located in Bottrop, Germany, this park (humorously enough) is themed to places that are, in fact, located in the United States, such as Hollywood and New York. Their lineup comes with a surplus of Vekoma coasters and family thrill rides that are rather inoffensive. *Star Trek: Operation Enterprise* is their headlining attraction; this is a Mack Rides launched coaster that (despite not being too impressive statistically speaking) is nevertheless a formidable coaster with a unique twisted vertical rollback. This park also has a license for Nickelodeon trademarks, and this bleeds into the attractions and theming as well.

- ### 65. Disney's Hollywood Studios

Okay, so here's the thing: this is the lucky Disney park in Florida that ended up receiving the Stars Wars Land when it opened in 2019. This alone puts this Disney theme park on the list. Of course, they still have the OG *Hollywood Tower of Terror,* which is nothing short of a classic.

- ## 64. Stratosphere

I was considering including this park in the top 50 just because of how insane of a destination this is. Over 1,100 feet in the air, these flat rides will spin you dangling over the side of the building, thrust you off the edge before brakes keep you from a plummet to your death, or launch you up and down a drop tower that gives you elevation above the clouds. Yep, this place is insane. They even have bungee jumping off the building; you might as well, huh?

- ## 63. Lagoon Amusement Park

This family-owned amusement park based in Utah has quite the charm beyond the vertical drop of a beast in the roller coaster, *Cannibal.* Beyond this, there isn't a well-rounded line-up, but the family-owned charm and solid collection of family coasters alongside make this a destination worth checking out.

Tip 47: Cannibal has a rare elevator lift system that thrusts riders up to the top of this tall, rather unique structure that serves as the centerpiece of this coaster.

- ## 62. Universal Studios Singapore

This Universal park, located in Singapore, has all your classic Universal favorites. *Revenge of the Mummy,* your indoor family, launched coaster; *Jurassic Park Rapids Adventure*, an exhilarating water ride that never gets old; as well as the *Transformers: The Ride 3D* dark ride. If I'm being honest, it's nothing too special for a Universal park, but it is a good park considering that all Universal parks *have* excellent theming and quality.

- ## 61. SeaWorld San Diego

This beautifully executed SeaWorld park has not just the classic Sea Lion comedy show that everyone can share a laugh with but also an ever-expanding lineup of roller coasters with the new addition of their B&M Dive Coaster *Emperor. Manta,* the multi-launched Mack Rides coaster, is also arguably one of the best family thrill coasters. Also: the penguins are cute. Go visit SeaWorld!

- ## 60. All boardwalk parks

I wanted to give a shoutout to each of the excellent boardwalk parks that are out there. They are mainly present in the U.S., with parks such as **Mori's Piers, Santa Cruz Beach Boardwalk, Kemah Boardwalk, Indiana Beach Boardwalk, and Galveston Island Historic Pleasure Pier.** Boardwalk parks have that carnival charm to them, with excellent games and funnel cakes. They'll literally sell fried anything too. Some of these boardwalk parks will even have a headlining roller coaster or two as well; Kemah Boardwalk is home to a bombshell of a Woodie named *"Boardwalk Bullet,"* for instance; it's one of the better creations by GCI out there. There is typically a good-looking Ferriss Wheel to go on as well, making these parks a top choice to go on a date, especially considering that visiting these parks is *also* visiting the beach at the same time. You'll also come across your classic, thrilling flats, just as if you were headed to the local carnival. Maybe you'll even find the house with the funny mirrors at some of these!

- ## 59. Parque de Atracions de Madrid

Although this may not be the most impressive park to make our list, it definitely has its perks and quirks. *Abismo* is one of the oddest roller coasters to the eye out there. Located in the "Machinery" section of the park, this rather uncomfortable (but in a good way) experience is immediately identifiable with its vertical lift hill that goes more than vertical at the end. At the same time, it releases riders when they are upside down. And that's just how the ride starts. This decently themed park has a good selection of family flats and thrills as well. In fact, *Abismo* is the only thrilling coaster at the park; the rest of their lineup is family oriented. Also: if your kiddos like Nickelodeon, this is another park with Nickelodeon theming with all the SpongeBob and Paw Patrol you could hope for.

- ## 58. Grona Lund

This amusement park, located in Stockholm, Sweden, may not be the largest park on this list, but it definitely has some excellent standout thrill coasters. *For example, Fritt Fall* is one of those drop towers I mentioned earlier that turns riders face down, and at the same time, they plummet towards the ground. In addition, *Twister* is a neat little woodie that families and even some thrill-seekers alike can appreciate, and *Monster*, their brand-new B&M Invert, is sure to be quite the crowd pleaser.

- **57. Holiday Park**

Being one of Germany's most popular theme parks, this well-kept park with quaint theming also boasts a few excellent roller coasters. One of them is a cloned Sky Rocket II model from premier rides, but the other is one of the best in the world. *Expedition G-Force,* which regularly competes for a top spot on the Golden Ticket Awards, is nothing short of an extreme Intamin hyper coaster that has some of the most intense airtime as well as laterals and overbank turns on a roller coaster.

Tip 48: The Golden Ticket Awards rank the best steel and wooden coasters every year. This award show also gives awards to parks based on different categories as this yearly event is hosted by a different park every year.

- **56. California Great America**

Located in Northern California, this park is host to one of the world's best wooden coasters, *Gold Striker*, a twisted GCI woodie known for its tunnels. They are also hosted by an RMC raptor, *RailBlazer,* as well as a unique B&M invert, *Flight Deck.* If you ever find yourself visiting Northern California, whether it's to catch a 49ers game or hit the beach, this park is definitely worth adding to your to-do list for the trip.

- **55. Six Flags Over Texas**

I was considering including this in the top 50 but wasn't able to find it a spot. Nevertheless, this park has a good selection of thrill coasters, including *Mr. Freeze Reverse Blast,* which has an inverting "top hat" loop and a wicked backward launch. They also have a few other legit thrill coasters that are worth checking out. This is the original Six Flags park, as although it may have the typical Six Flags cookie cutter theming, it's still got a lot to offer to guests.

Tip 49: There is also the New Texas Giant, which is the O.G RMC hybrid coaster that, is the only RMC roller coaster not to feature any inversions since it was their first project of this kind.

- **54. Six Flags Mexico**

In the heart of Mexico City is Six Flags Mexico, which has the reputation of actually being a pretty park with wonderful charm and heritage. Their roller coaster collection is also pretty legit, with a one-two punch of *Superman El Ultimo Escape,* an Intamin hyper coaster, as well as *Medusa Steel Coaster,* which is another earlier RMC hybrid. All in all, I'd also say this is a pretty good park for the whole family as well; it's definitely worth checking out.

Tip 50: Medusa Steel Coaster was the first RMC to feature a zero-G roll first drop in which riders head down the first hill while simultaneously experiencing the ride's first inversion.

- **53. Mirabiliandia**

Here's some more representation straight out of Savio, Italy. Mirabilandia is home to the world-famous *iSpeed*, which is a launched Intamin Blitz coaster that launches riders at 68 mph in 2.2 seconds while riders also experience two inversions, including an inline twist. The park also has arguably one of the best B&M

Inverts in Europe in *Katun.* The park also tries to be well-rounded with family attractions and shows. Also, this is yet another European park where Nickelodeon theming is present.

Tip 51: Inline twists are inversions that will literally twist 360 degrees and create a full 360 roll, which also means they look just as cool as they feel while riding.

- **52. Erlebnispark Tripsdill**

Despite my gripes with trying to discern how to pronounce the name of this German park, this doesn't take away from the fact that it does have a lot to offer. Almost enough to land itself a spot in the top 50, if I'm being honest. The park has a theme park, a wildlife park, and a nature resort. This gorgeous park property, with tons of green, is also home to *Karacho,* a launched Gerstalauer Euro-Fighter with four inversions.

- **51. Blackpool Pleasure Beach**

Blackpool Pleasure Beach claims to be "The UK's most ride-intensive amusement park." Now, although this may be yet another European park that has a fascination with Nickelodeon theming, they may not be wrong in stating that they are, in fact, a ride-intensive amusement park. After all, they *are* home to the steel hyper coaster, *The Big One,* as well as the steel double, launched coaster in *Icon.* This Mack Rides launched coaster is smooth and even a bit intense, as it sits with its 82ft. tall top hat and lone inversion with its even taller 85ft. Immelmann loop.

- **50. Kennywood**

Tip 52: Phantom's Revenge, the intense airtime filled hyper coaster which, has a larger and better second drop than a first drop, and Steel Curtain steal (no pun intended) the show at this park, which is located in Pennsylvania.

Steel Curtain has nine inversions and is manufactured by S&S, as the ride is actually themed to the Pittsburg Steelers. This was a part of a newly themed section *to* the Pittsburg Steelers. I also would like to mention their old dinosaur of a wooden coaster, *Jack Rabbit,* which is a lovable, yet some consider painful, classic.

Whew, okay. Time for a quick breather. Each of these parks is worth a visit if you happen to be in the area. But now we'll move on to the parks that *"are"* you visit. These are the kind of parks that coaster enthusiasts will hop on a plane to travel to.

This top 49 is also ranked from 49 – 1. Are you ready?

Parks Ranked 49 – 11

- **49. Ferrari World**

In Abu Dhabi, United Arab Emirates is "Ferrari's Branded Theme Park," Ferrari World. According to their website, they also claim to be the largest indoor theme park to exist. The park most certainly sits in an incredibly constructed red structure with a Ferrari logo on the roof that can be seen by planes flying overhead.

Tip 53: In fact, they actually have an attraction in which you take a 90-minute walk across the roof. It's appropriately titled Roof Walk.

They are also home to other family Ferrari-themed attractions, as well as *Flying Aces,* which is a steel Intamin winged coaster that is home to the world's tallest non-inverting loop. Fortunately, this isn't the world record that draws folks to this park. They are also home to the world's fastest roller coaster, yes, *the* fastest roller coaster to exist. *Formula Rossa,* which sits outside the building, launches riders at 149 mph in 4.9 seconds. Since 2010, this coaster has held this record.

- ## 48. Walibi Holland

Lost Gravity (a unique Mack Rides "Big Dipper" modeled coaster that is themed to Gravity and gives great negative G-forces), *Goliath* (an Intamin Mega Coaster with an excellent layout), and *Untamed* (their new RMC hybrid) are their main draws to bring in guests. And let me just say, this is an excellent top three. Walibi Holland used to be owned by Six Flags, although, since the ownership change, an up in the quality of the park is noticeable. Nevertheless, this park should deliver a fun time for you and your party, and that's why it barely cracked the top 50.

- ## 47. King's Dominion

King's Dominion is another excellent park that is home to one of the most unreal coasters, *Intimidator 305,* which rips riders apart with G-force, as this Intamin Giga coaster is unique in what it offers compared to the others. Their RMC, *Twisted Timbers,* is also one of the better RMCs in the country. They also have a great selection of family coasters and attractions. Their lineup is the most well-rounded roller coaster lineup on this list thus far, in my opinion. The park is also seemingly making an effort to improve the theming and storyline of the different themed lands of the park, so keep a lookout for the lore here in the park's future.

- ## 46. Knoebles

Okay, so maybe this park is slightly overrated. After all, it doesn't have that complete coaster lineup like Kings Dominion or even Walibi Holland have. But what this family park, located in Elysburg, Pennsylvania, does have is a lot of charm and a lot of trees. In fact, they even have a campground. Sign me up for that! They are also home to the famous airtime-filled woodie, *Phoenix,* which may not impress with a glance at the statistics, but it most definitely is worth riding for yourself to see what all the hype is about. They also have their unique wooden bobsled *Flying Turns,* which we discussed earlier, as well as *Impulse,* their first major steel roller coaster that inverts riders four times and has a vertical drop. This is also an excellent park to bring the family; the family-owned park atmosphere is different and in a good way.

Tip 54: What makes this park also stand out from the rest is the fact that park admission is FREE. Yes, FREE. You pay for the rides, similar to that of a carnival, and NOT by admission. Isn't that awesome?

- **45. Six Flags New England**

Some, not all, but some argue this park has the best one-two punch in the United States. I suppose it's a bit of a taste discussion. Six Flags New England is home to *Superman The Ride, one* of *the* best Intamin hyper coasters out there, and Wicked Cyclone, a short but incredibly powerful RMC hybrid coaster worth the trip to the park alone. The reason I can't rank the park any higher is that the lineup of coasters drops off a bit from there, but it's safe to say (for me at least) that their one-two punch is good enough to carry them to number 45 on the list.

- **44. Tivoli Gardens**

This park is insanely gorgeous and completely immersive. Quite frankly, I suggest you look up photos of this park and the various themed areas, and you'll be impressed. The coaster selection is nothing to shout about, but they have a good selection of family rides, as this seems to be the objective of the park. The park pays attention to how everything looks at this park, even the flat rides (which they do have a decent little collection of, even thrill flats). The park has been described as "a playground for the young and old," as this "playground" was built in 1843, as it's the most popular park in Scandinavia. For these reasons and more, Tivoli Gardens scores at number 44 on the list.

- ## 43. Disneyland Paris

Disneyland Paris, it's Disneyland, but in Paris. So what else is there to say? Well, contrary to the original Disneyland, they named their futuristic land "Discoveryland," and quite frankly, it looks a bit cooler than Tomorrowland. Other than that, there isn't too much that makes this park any different that's worth mentioning, other than little details or attractions here and there. Obviously, you'll know what to expect with Disneyland, excellent theming, storytelling, and beauty.

- ## 42. Toverland

Located in Kronenburg, Netherlands, Toverland is home to a great GCI woodie, *Troy*, as well as a B&M winged coaster, *Fenix*. It's becoming no secret that each of these European parks that have been making an appearance on this top 50 is nothing short of stunning, and this simple fact is no different with Toverland. Toverland isn't just an average well-themed park. It miraculously pulls off interesting lands such as "Ithaka," an Ancient Greek-inspired section of the park, as well as their new "Avalon," which is based on Celtic mythology. They also have a superb collection of water rides and some family-oriented thrill coasters and flats.

- ## 41. Hansa-Park

Hansa-Park is another German theme park to crack the list, and guess what? It's also well-themed and beautiful. What a surprise. They are home to a couple of interesting Gerstlauer coasters, which make up their top two. Both of which have one inversion and are well-themed coasters. *The Escape of Novgorod* even includes small dark ride portions before it launches riders at 62 mph and whips riders through a series of intense elements before going up another lift hill (a vertical one) and dropping riders at 97 degrees; all indoors and in the dark, I might add. Watch a POV of this ride; it's quite a trip. This is what Hansa-Park does so well, which is what gives it its spot on this list. The rides are well-themed and executed.

- **40. Disney's California Adventure**

Tip 55: Across from Disneyland sits this park, which was initially intended to be more of an adult park to counteract Disney when it opened in the year 2001. Here you'll find the classic "Paradise Pier," which hosts the Incredicoaster and Mickey's Fun Wheel.

In addition, their incredible "Cars Land," which is home to *Radiator Springs Racers* and various other family-based dark rides and attractions, is nothing short of a lineup of classics, considering Disney seems to just open up nothing but classics in the public eye.

- **39. Gardaland**

With a one-two punch of a B&M winged and dive coaster, this well-themed park in northeast Italy has an Arabian-themed area, a Western-themed area, a Medieval-themed area, and a family-based area themed to Kung fu Panda (Kung fu Panda Academy). In 2022, Gardaland also opened up *Jumanji-The Adventure,* their first interactive dark ride, which is another must-ride at the park.

- **38. Thorpe Park**

Thorpe Park has such a rad collection of roller coasters. *Nemesis Inferno* is an excellent B&M Invert; The *Swarm* is a highly regarded winged coaster; *SAW--The Ride* is a well-themed and intricate Euro-Fighter with a 100-degree drop. And *Stealth,* which is an Intamin launched coaster that is the fastest in the UK, going 0 to 80 mph in 2.5 seconds. The park is located in Chertsey, Surrey, which is near London. They brand themselves as "The UK's Most Thrilling Theme Park," and I'd say they may not only fit in the theme park category, but they may also just be the UK's most thrilling park.

- ## 37. Kolmarden

This wildlife park that sits south of Stockholm is host to countless animals, beautiful scenery, and one of the best wooden roller coasters in the world, which comes in the form of RMC's ground-up project, *Wildfire*. Their animal displays and shows are second to none.

Tip 56: If visiting the park, I highly recommend you reserve a spot for you and your party on the Safari gondola, which is their Safari, but on a cableway. It's the only cableway Safari I've come across.

- ## 36. SeaWorld Orlando

Here is the third highest animal-based park to crack our top 50. What separates the Orlando park from the rest? That would be their incredible one-two punch of *Mako*, their B&M hyper coaster, and *Manta*, their B&M flying coaster. This park also has your typical collection of SeaWorld experiences and shows. However, I do intend some humor with this.

Tip 57: Beware when visiting parks in Florida; the summertime humidity makes it difficult for residents of less humid climates to complain about the weather and take constant breaks in the middle of the afternoon.

- ## 35. Energylandia

Energylandia has quite the big-boy coasters, including *Zadra,* a demented 200-foot-tall RMC; *Hyperion,* an Intamin Mega Coaster that touches 88 miles per hour and even has a single inversion; and Vekoma's first "Space Warp launched coaster," which includes three inversions.

Tip 58: Despite the stigma surrounding the Dutch company Vekoma, and their less favorable older rides, the company's new generation of coasters are reported to be much smoother and quite excellent rides.

- ## 34. Port Aventura World

We discussed Ferrari land earlier, which sits by Port Aventura World... the main draw. They are home to the intense *Furius Baco,* a unique launched winged coaster by Intamin that touches 83.9 miles per hour and has one inversion, as well as the amazing *Shambala,* a world-renowned B&M hyper coaster with incredible airtime, as well as *Dragon Khan. This picturesque B&M floorless coaster* sits by and throws riders for eight inversions. This floorless coaster is actually one of the taller ones, too. All in all, they also have a good selection of family attractions. This park is well-rounded with its amazing one-two-three punch.

- ## 33. Glenwood Caverns

This is the most unique park to crack the top 50 list. Allow me to help you understand why. Glenwood Caverns is located in Glenwood Springs, Colorado. Not only do they have caves you can visit, but they also have some awesome thrill rides. You see, the park is located at the top of a mountain, and it uses the terrain to the park's advantage. *Giant Canyon Swing* is your typical Screamin' Swing flat ride by S&S, except it sits off the edge of the mountain, and you face nothing but a huge drop-off below while facing down at the canyon below. The *Haunted Mine Drop* is quite possibly the most impressive attraction they have, which is an indoor drop tower that catches riders by surprise when they drop in the dark in this insane mine-themed attraction that is a must-ride. Their new *Defiance Roller Coaster* is their new action-packed Gerstlauer Euro-Fighter, which possesses a 102.3-degree free fall drop. The park also has a charming collection of family attractions that complement this lineup of rides making this a must-travel to.

- ## 32. Universal Studios Orlando

The Florida park is home to *Hollywood Rip Ride Rocket* and seems to have a different (some consider for the better) Harry Potter World than the Hollywood park (the Orlando Park has the fire-breathing dragon overlooking Diagon Alley). The Orlando park does everything better than the Hollywood park (for the most part). However, I decided to rank it lower because it doesn't have the unique Hollywood-like experience and Studio Tour, which is why you'll see Hollywood higher up on our list. Nevertheless, it's important to discuss why this Universal park does rank so high on this list. It still has all the classic Universal attractions like *Transformers the Ride, Revenge of the Mummy,* and even *Despicable Me Minion Mayhem.*

- **31. Canada's Wonderland**

Canada's Wonderland is easily the most impressive park that calls Canada its home. With a solid top three of their B&M Giga and Hyper, *Leviathan* and *Behemoth,* they are also host to a B&M Dive Coaster, *Yukon Striker,* and a myriad of other thrill but also family attractions.

Tip 59: Do not ride Time Warp, their painful little flying coaster made by Zamperla. Do not be enticed by short lines, folks; they are short for a reason. At the same time, long lines are long for a reason, typically a really good one.

This park is also known for having a well-rounded collection of thrilling flat rides, but really just a lot of rides in general and a lot to do here in general. They even have an interactive 4D dark ride in their famous Wonder Mountain named *Wonder Mountain's Guardian,* which is a neat ride with even a coaster track section.

- **30. Six Flags Great America**

Six Flags Great America has quite the coaster collection to boast about. This park makes quite a few other Six Flags parks jealous of the attention that this one gets.

Tip 60: Be aware that large chains like Six Flags and Cedar Fair do give certain parks more attention than others. If your home park hasn't received anything new or exciting in the past five to ten years, has received re-located attractions from other parks, or if you suspect the park is being run in a poor manner, this, unfortunately, may be the case with your home park.

Six Flags Great America is home to *Goliath. This RMC wooden coaster* is nothing short of an intense ride with elements that pack a punch, *X-Flight,* a neat little B&M winged coaster; *Raging Bull,* a unique twister B&M hyper coaster; *Superman Ultimate Flight,* a clone layout of an enjoyable yet thrilling B&M flyer; and *Maxx Force, their* new Premier Rides launched coaster that hits 78 miles per hour.

Tip 61: Maxx Force has the world's fastest inversion, a zero-G roll at 60 miles per hour, as well as the world's tallest double inversion at 175 feet tall. As you can tell, this park is nothing short of awesome.

- **29. Disney's Animal Kingdom**

Here is the second highest animal park to crack our list, which is yet another Disney World park to make an appearance on our list. *Pandora – The World of Avatar* is an incredible themed area that is breathtaking; just go check out photos of it! They also have a neat collection of animals and are also home to *Expedition Everest,* which literally may just be the line between family and thrill coaster. The ride's indoor section has this backward helix that was far more intense than I was expecting, and the ride and mountain are well landscaped and quite immersive. All in all, this is a must-visit, especially if you decide to visit Disney World. It's a beautiful park that accomplishes its objective for guests visiting the park.

- **28. Universal Studios Japan**

Yes, I did rank Universal Studios Japan higher than the Florida one because, quite frankly, it has more to offer, in my opinion. The park has *Flying Dinosaur*, which may be the best B&M flying coaster ever to exist. It also has all of your other Universal classics and theming, as well as even more rides and attractions because the Japan park just seems to go above and beyond. It is also ironic how both the Florida and Japan park have roller coasters themed to Hollywood, but the park in Hollywood doesn't. Their Hollywood park, *Hollywood Dream Coaster,* is a B&M model that may not hit the 200ft mark but definitely does supply classic B&M airtime-filled rides.

- **27. Heide Park**

Heide Park is yet another beautiful and well-themed park located in Soltau, Germany. *Colossos – Kampf der Giganten* is an incredible wooden coaster with this centerpiece of a giant beast-looking wooden creature that has fire shooting out of its head and breathing smoke as the track rips through the palm of his hand. The Intamin woodie also happens to be 164 feet tall and has an intense layout.

Tip 62: It was the first wooden coaster to use this prefabricated track technology.

They are also hosted by *KRAKE,* an awesome-looking B&M dive coaster, as well as *Flug der Damonen,* which is another B&M winged coaster that does a good job of rounding out this park's lineup. The park's specialty, however, would still be considered the theming and landscape, as they are even able to execute such things throughout the course of their thrill rides which is exceptionally difficult and shows the park indeed cares and pays attention to the details.

- **26. Disney's Magic Kingdom**

This park is a classic. Almost as classic as the original Disneyland. Nevertheless, Disney's Magic Kingdom comes set with all your classic Disney favorites, including your trio of Mountain coasters.

Magic Kingdom is set with parades, fireworks, live shows, character meet and greets, and the whole enchilada. The full experience lands this family-oriented park high up and the list.

- **25. Efteling**

Efteling brands itself is a "World of Wonder," and quite frankly, they have every reason to be considering how extensive and serious they take their immersive qualities to the park. I find this park to be especially impressive with how well done it is. *Fata Morgana* and *Symbolica* (go check out their POVs) are both world-class dark rides, and *Baran 1989* is another well-themed European B&M dive coaster. The storytelling aspects of this park's attraction are intriguing, as this fantasy-themed land is so well done that you very well may feel like you are living in the fantasy the park has prepared for you.

- **24. Tokyo Disneyland**

I've covered quite a few parks similar to this already, Disney has continuously made appearances on this list, and by the end of this list, all the Disneyland parks will have made their appearance on this list. What more is there to say about these parks? They have all your classic Disney attractions, coasters, and dark rides. Obviously, each park has its own variations of certain attractions and such.

- **23. Busch Gardens Tampa**

Not only does Busch Gardens Tampa come set with animals such as Elephants, Giraffes, Penguins, and Tigers, but they are also home to one of the most stacked coaster lineups a park could possibly offer. *Iron Gwazi* is their enormous RMC steel brute with a wicked layout; *Montu* is a favorite B&M Invert of many; Cheetah Hunt is a triple launched coaster that may have been intended to be a family coaster but still may intimidate them a bit too much. The park itself is well kept and, well, pretty well themed. This is a must-travel to in my opinion.

- **22. Liseberg**

Go check out a POV of *Helix*. *It's* a coaster that utilizes the terrain and has seven incredible inversions. The layout is a bit unconventional but in the best way. Liseberg has a very well-rounded collection of rides, with standout coasters that make it another must-travel to park. They, too, have a B&M dive coaster; it seems like these European parks truly can't get enough of these things.

- **21. Six Flags Fiesta Texas**

This quite possibly might be the best-themed and most well-kept Six Flags park to exist. I didn't say it was *the best*, but it definitely is close. The park sits by a quarry wall which gives it a beautiful backdrop that is even utilized with the layouts of a few of their best rides like *Iron Rattler* (their RMC steel hybrid), as well as *Superman Krypton Coaster*, which is widely considered to be the best B&M floorless coaster out there. In 2022, they are also opening the world's steepest Dive Coaster, *Dr. Diabolical's Cliffhanger.*

Tip 63: This was the first park to host two RMC roller coasters, the Iron Rattler AND Wonder Women Golden Lasso Coaster, their single rail modeled coasters.

- **20. Busch Gardens Williamsburg**

Busch Gardens Williamsburg is also home to an absolutely loaded lineup of coasters. *Pantheon* is a coaster with four launches and a 95 degrees drop. They have a trio of good B&Ms in *Griffon, Apollo's Chariot,* and *Alpengiest.*

Tip 64: Alpengiest is the only B&M Invert to reach the 200-foot mark, making it a hyper coaster.

Verbolten is a partially indoors, partially outdoors coaster with a strong storyline that thrills riders and has a unique drop track. The park is very pretty and is themed in various European countries. European parks tend to be gorgeous, so leave it to us Americans to just copy them to make a pretty park. This may very well be the most stunning park in the United States.

- **19. Nagashima Spa Land**

Not only are they home to the massive and world-famous *Steel Dragon 2000*, which has a track length of over 8,000 feet, or the rather quirky *Ultra Twister* that has flips riders in a unique looking manner, but they also are home to ten other coasters as this Japanese park that sits on the beautiful coast of the ocean. They are also home to the *Aurora Wheel,* a nearly 300 ft. tall Ferris Wheel, quite the impressive attraction if you ask me that it has an excellent capacity. So, not only is there a solid lineup of coasters and flats here but it is rounded out with beautiful scenery and a wonderful atmosphere. Good enough to the extent this Nagashima Spa Land cracks our top 20.

- **18. Six Flags Great Adventure**

The only thing that holds this park back is the fact that Six Flags run the park. However, the coaster lineup itself is one of the best in the world, including *Kingda Ka* (the world's tallest coaster), *El Toro* (an Intamin Woodie that slaps), *Nitro* (a B&M hyper coaster), and *Jersey Devil* (an RMC single rail coaster). The park also has a Safari, which is a plus, and something you wouldn't really expect in this instance. All in all, this park has a really good collection of rides and a lineup that is deep and has depth.

- **17. Epcot**

Tip 65: The Epcot World Showcase has pavilions or "showcases" presenting 11 different countries such as Japan, France, and even Italy.

The world showcase alone is a reason for Epcot to be viewed in high regard as a must-travel to park. In case you didn't know, the park itself is a gem, a historical one at that. *Mission Space,* the classic dark ride, sits in the giant golf ball, which is the iconic centerpiece of the park. They are also home to *Test Track,* which reaches speeds of 65 miles per hour and has Tron-like dark ride elements themed to testing the car you designed in the queue before getting on to ride. The park is also continuously making improvements, which inclines me to rank Disney parks higher on the list in many instances because the company is always installing new and even more innovative attractions than their predecessors, which is why Epcot ranks at 17.

- **16. Knott's Berry Farm**

Not only does Knott's have one of the world's best wooden coasters, *Ghost Rider,* which has excellent laterals and a long, drawn out (in the best way possible) layout, but they also are home to *Xcelerator,* which goes 82 miles per hour in 2.3 seconds. Each themed section of the park is also well-done, and the park is beautiful.

Tip 66: Be sure to also spend quality time in Ghost Town, an old western town in the middle of the park, rich with history and, in some seasons, has live actors. Ghost Town has old western shops, food places, and even a Blacksmith. The town was initially built for guests to enjoy while they waited for their World-famous Knott's chicken dinner, but eventually, the whole park followed suit.

The boardwalk section of the park is also excellent, and the lights and atmosphere are second to none. The park has a classic log ride, train, and mine ride (*Calico Mine Co.*), which each contribute to the park's extensive history and classic charm.

- **15. Disneyland**

In my opinion, the park itself standing alone would not necessarily crack a top 20. But for the sake of history, experience, and for the sake of Walt Disney himself, it's only respectful to award Disneyland a high spot on the list for the path it paved for the industry as a whole. For the innovation that will go without ceasing, and the landmarks and milestones that make this park simultaneously on the cutting edge, but also the essence of classic and nostalgia. Throughout the book, I've made countless references to this park; after all, most people know the references I'm making and know all the classic attractions that the park has to offer. So for these reasons alone, and the giant turkey legs, of course, Disneyland will sit here at number 15.

- **14. Carowinds**

Okay, back to roller coasters. Carowinds, in recent years, has been heavily invested in as it now has one of the better roller coaster collections in the world. *Fury 325* is widely considered to be the best Giga coaster yet, *Afterburn* is an intense B&M invert that causes many to grey out, and *Copperhead Strike* is their new double-launched coaster that has five excellent inversions. The park also crosses both North and South Carolina. Other than the top end of their roller coaster lineup, they also have a solid enough collection of thrill flats and family flats. Nothing too noteworthy, but still, it's important to consider before a trip here.

- **13. Universal Studios Hollywood**

If you happen to be a movie enthusiast, Universal Studios Hollywood may be a park of even higher importance on this list compared to what's ahead, considering it sits here at number 13. I previously discussed the *World-Famous Studio Tour* and *The Wizarding World of Harry Potter* because they have already been noteworthy enough in the book and in the context of the best that the amusement and theme park industry has to offer. Your experience here will be filled with movie-like atmospheres, laughs, entertainment, and thrills. This park offers a movie experience unlike any other movie-themed park because of its location, right in the heart of Hollywood, and for the history and relics, the park will always have on display.

- ## 12. Islands of Adventure

Islands of Adventure is the definition of quality over quantity. Their headlining attractions are nothing short of the best of the best. They are home to *Hagrid's Magical Creatures Motorbike Adventure* (the most expensive but also most elaborately themed thrill ride to date), *Incredible Hulk* (a classic B&M floorless coaster that is unlike any other), and *Velocicoasater* (which many consider to be their favorite roller coaster ever built, we'll discuss this ride in the next chapter). The theming at this park is also as good as a Universal park could be. As we mentioned earlier, the park is host to the magical *Hogsmeade*, while Universal park has *Diagon Alley*. The park also is home to other mythical lands like Suess Landing, Jurassic Park, and Marvel Superhero Land, which is home to the brilliant *The Amazing Adventures of Spiderman,* which we'll also discuss later.

- ## 11. Phantasialand

This would be widely considered to be the best park in Germany if it wasn't for one other park that will be making an appearance higher up on our list. The park pays lots of attention to detail when it comes to the theming of their various lands and even their roller coasters. In fact, I'd go as far as to say no other park (with the exception of a few) does a better job theming their coasters than Phantasialand. Their lands, Berlin, Mexico, China Town, Mystery, Fantasy, and Deep in Africa, are all impressive. *Black Mamba* is an excellent B&M Invert, and *Taron* is an Intamin multi-launched coaster that features a 73-mile-per-hour *launch and a layout that winds through the incredible landscape and themed* structures; the theming is second to none. No other ride does it better than this, and I actually mean that.

All in all, the park also has a larger than usual collection of water rides, each of which is great. I'd also consider this to be a perfect park for families to visit. I'd say the fact that this park can so easily

attract both families and coaster enthusiasts are what scores
Phantasialand such a high ranking on our list.

Parks Ranked 10 – 1

- **10. Tokyo Disney Sea**

This fantasy theme park has breathtaking landscaping and theming.
I could not rave enough about each themed section of this park.
Mount Prometheus is the centerpiece of the park, a giant volcano
that does, in fact, burst fire. It sits on Mysterious Island, which has
this incredible looking rock façade that is gorgeous to the eye. The
Mediterranean Harbor has actual ports, Mermaid Lagoon displays
colors and vibrancy I never thought possible, and Arabian Coast
contains that signature Arabic architecture that Disney parks seem
to do well at. They have excellent headline attractions in the form of
their dark rides, *Journey to the Center of the Earth*, and *Raging
Spirits,* this neat family coaster that sits in Ancient Ruins. A few
attractions in this park will also be mentioned later in this book, as
bucket list rides you need to add to the list.

- **9. Silver Dollar City**

This park has an old, rustic, woodsy kind of charm to it. This
beautiful park is filled with trees and natural beauty. They have a
few notable attractions, such as *Outlaw Run*, an RMC Woodie with
a viral double heartline roll, and an excellent layout that has that
signature RMC airtime. *Time Traveler* offers a different experience
each time guests ride it, as this spinning coaster features two
launches, a 90-degree drop, and three inversions. The food at this
park is also delicious, and the thrill, as well as family attraction
lineups, are equally excellent. This adventurous park embodies
what a well-rounded American theme park should be like.

- **8. Fuji-Q Highland**

What makes this park rank at number 8? It could be a number of things; perhaps it's *Eejanaika,* the 4D coaster that learned from the few mistakes of the prototype, *X2.* Maybe it is the 112-mile-per-hour launch on *Do Dodonpa* or the 62-mile-per-hour launching coaster in *Takabisha* that has seven inversions as well as a 121-degree drop. This top-loaded lineup deserves a spot in our top ten for this reason alone. The park prides itself on having an array of "world's best" attractions and on fair reasoning.

Tip 67: When Takabisha opened, it had the steepest drop in the world. Unfortunately, TMNT Shellraiser at Nickelodeon Universe at American Dream eventually broke the record by half a degree.

- **7. Six Flags Magic Mountain**

Tip 68: With 20 roller coasters, Six Flags Magic Mountain has more roller coasters than any other theme park.

This is less of a family park and very much a concrete steel factory thrill seeker's paradise. Whether it's the 4D coaster, *X2,* the (sometimes racing and airtime filled) RMC, *Twisted Colossus,* or the B&M flyer, *Tatsu,* that has the most intense pretzel loop on a flying coaster as it rips through the trees of the mountain, Six Flags has an absolute stacked lineup of coasters. The only reason the park isn't higher is that it's run like a Six Flags park. There is a lack of cleanliness and charm. But if you are a coaster enthusiast who only cares about visiting parks with the most thrills, then this park may very well be in your top three.

- **6. Hershey Park**

Hershey Park is, unfortunately, the only chocolate-themed park on the list, but at least it debuts here at number 6. Residing in Hershey, Pennsylvania, Hershey Park is home to an exciting group of coasters, including the B&M hyper, *Candymonium,* the Intamin hyper, *Skyrush,* the Intamin Accelerator coaster, *Storm Runner,* and *Great Bear,* a B&M layout with a quirky layout. All in all, this lineup is deep, but the park's ranking isn't high just for the collection of coasters or the fact that it also has an extensive collection of family coasters (like the spinning indoor coaster *Laugh Track,* which deserves a quick shoutout), flats, and attractions. No, this park is also home to unique candy-themed attractions.

Tip 69: Outside of the park itself sits Hershey's Chocolate World Attraction, where guests can take a free tour ride of the chocolate factory, there's a 4D chocolate mystery show, and guests even have the opportunity to create their own candy bar. I find the creative names of rides, being themed to chocolate bars, also to be a good touch.

- **5. King's Island**

This park is home to one of, if not the, best GCI wooden coaster, *Mystic Timbers,* which has an out and back layout that refuses to quit. The park is also home to a trio of incredible B&M coasters with their Giga *Orion,* hyper *Diamondback,* and terrifying B&M invert *Banshee.*

Tip 70: Diamondback has a splash-down ending, in which the track sits in a small body of water, creating a giant splash when the vehicle runs through that portion of the ride, serving as a way to slow the train down like a brake.

The park is also home to *The Beast,* which has over 7,000 feet of track and a unique old layout as the park itself manufactured the ride. This park is also pretty well-rounded, with a good selection of rides for each family member, even the little ones. The park also is well-kept and has good landscaping, which is a plus. Nevertheless, this park is mostly a priority for coaster enthusiasts first, which it is a must-travel to.

- ## 4. Dollywood

Dollywood has everything together, an excellent selection of thrill coasters, family coasters, thrill flats, family flats, good food, entertaining shows, as well as a warm and woodsy atmosphere (as it sits in Pigeon Forge, Tennessee). They are home to *Lightning Rod,* an intense airtime filled launched wooden coaster; *Tennessee Tornado,* a timeless classic that hasn't lost its power reaching speeds of 70 miles per hour and thrilling inversions; and a collection of other coasters that finish off this well-rounded lineup. *Fire Chaser Express* may very well be the world's best family coaster, with excellent theming and even a backwards section. The park has different seasonal events, each offering something different and charming. The park also has a collection of dining shows in which guests dine and eat, which quite frankly isn't something every park offers. The park has 11 themed lands. Including "Rivertown Junction" and "Wildwood Grove." The park seems to truly honor its history as well, as Dolly Parton herself probably is never bored visiting the park she had once imagined.

- ## 3. Alton Towers

This is the park that gives Phantasialand competition for which park themes their roller coasters best. Due to its location (Staffordshire, England), Alton Towers has height restrictions for how tall they can build their coasters. Fortunately, this only has made the park better and more creative with each ride's layout and how the terrain is often utilized. *For example, nemesis* is a tight and intense B&M Invert, *The Smiler* has more inversions (14) than any other coaster, and *Oblivion* is a B&M dive coaster that sits in the "X-Sector" of the park.

Tip 71: Oblivion may only be 65 feet tall, but it features a drop of 180 feet, which means over 100 feet of the drop happen underground and in the dark. How cool is that?!

Because of the unique qualities and theming of their coasters, Alton Towers lands itself a top spot on our list.

- ## 2. Cedar Point

Cedar Point is known as "America's Roller Coast" for a good reason. Cedar Point is widely considered to have the deepest coaster lineup ever assembled. Where do I start? And which ride is the best? Is it *Millennium Force,* the Giga coaster that has won the most "Best steel coaster" by the Golden Ticket Awards? Is it *Maverick,* the intense Intamin Blitz coaster with the whippiest elements? Is it *Top Thrill Dragster,* the Stratocaster with arguably the world's best launch at 121 miles per hour, or is it *Steel Vengeance,* the brute of an RMC that resides in a daunting manner that has powerful blown-up elements followed by a tight and intense second half?

Tip 72: The coaster has more seconds of airtime than any other coaster, with nearly 30 seconds of it!

The park has more coasters over 200 feet tall than any other park, as the park has a beautiful skyline sitting on a peninsula in lucky Sandusky, Ohio. The fact that the park sits surrounded by a body of water truly adds to the atmosphere and gives it its charm. For these reasons, Cedar Point has deservingly found itself at number 2 on our list.

- ## Europa Park

We've finally made it to our top destination, and no park could be as deserving as Europa Park. Europa Park is well-rounded. What makes this park so great is that it will excite anyone who attends. Are you a thrill seeker? Europa Park is home to *Silver Star,* a dazzling 240-foot-tall B&M hyper coaster, *and Blue Fire Megacoaster*—a Mack Rides launched coaster that features four inversions as well as a brilliant dark ride section before it launches riders at 62 miles per hour with a theatrical soundtrack playing the whole time, as well as *WODAN – Timburcoaster,* which is a GCI wooden coaster with an excellent layout that ranks amongst the best. Want family attractions and rides? Well, Europa Park has a full arsenal of them, including *ARTHUR – The Ride,* an inverted spinning dark ride coaster that is perfect for the whole family. Want theming? You'll get the cream of the crop European park theming here; it'll be an immersive experience, unlike any other park. Want beauty? There is no corner in this park that isn't breathtakingly beautiful.

Tip 73: It is no surprise that Europa Park has recently been winning the "best park" category for the Golden Ticket Awards every year, dethroning Cedar Point, which consistently would win beforehand.

Europa Park has various themed lands that are themed to the various countries in Europe. Think of the Epcot World Showcase but blown up into a full park with (sorry, Epcot) more elaborate features and better (it's not even close) rides. France is often described as the most beautiful of the countries, and the food is (of course) really good here. Ireland is the section of the park that is generally seen as the kid's area, where you'll find all your attractions for the little ones. Rust, Germany is the lucky home to this park, and quite frankly, I've never heard anyone who visited this park and *hasn't* been blown away. The immersion at this park is the best that the industry has to offer. There is a mystical magic to this park that is often described from being here. For these reasons and more, Europa Park is our number one park.

Perhaps you were cheering for your home park to rank higher, or maybe you were surprised that one park was ranked above another. The reality is that each of our lists would be different if everyone were to create their own. Although I attempted to be objective with my rankings on this list and how I consider parks to be placed, this is definitely not to be viewed as *the* objectively best parks. After all, we all have different tastes. Be sure to visit some of these parks at some point in your life. Hopefully, one (or a few) even happens to be within driving distance!

Chapter 4: Fun roller coasters you should add to that bucket list of yours

We've now reviewed the top 101 parks you should probably check out if you ever get the chance to, but for some, that's not enough. Coaster enthusiasts are typically more about the individual ride experiences. They will go as far as to visit a park just to experience their singular standout coaster, even if the rest of the park is just mediocre. Nevertheless, each of these coasters that I urge you to ride someday are all at parks worth visiting, which all made our list in the previous chapter. So, here are some roller coasters you must add to your bucket list.

X2 (Six Flags Magic Mountain, California)

Type: Steel

Model: 4th Dimension

Height: 190' (215 ft. first drop)

Top Speed: 76 mph

Track Length: 3,610 ft.

Manufacturer: Arrow Dynamics

Six Flags Magic Mountain opened up "X" in 2002 as the world's first 4D coaster. Riders sit on the side of the track in a winged formation, two riders on each side.

Tip 74: The coaster basically has two sets up the track, one for the ride vehicle to follow, and the other controls the rotation of the vehicles. A rack and pinion mechanism is used to move the seats. It's quite an innovative concept that is best explained through researching photos rather than being explained in words.

In 2008, the ride reopened with a rebrand of "X2," which, quite frankly, was much better. Rather than a pink and yellow color scheme, the ride now had this menacing black and red color scheme that came with onboard audio, smoke, and fire effects. This is what truly sets this ride apart from others. The ride experience itself is incredibly intense, with a first drop that is nearly vertical in which the seats flip riders to face directly towards the ground while plummeting 215 feet; there is nothing else like it. Towards the end of the drop, riders flip head over heels into the next element, which is this enormous raven turn reversal element. The elements are quite difficult to explain, considering the 360 degrees seats may have riders inverted to the track, above the track, moving forwards, moving backward, or even simply just doing flips.

The whole thing is quite disorienting, especially for those who don't know what to expect before the ride starts.

Tip 75: The ride was designed by Alan Schilke, who is now at the head of designing rides for RMC. Tip: X2 gets incredibly long lines, considering it is a crowd favorite at Magic Mountain. Either be prepared to wait or get straight to X2 once the park opens.

Personally speaking, X2 is my all-time favorite coaster, the intimidating Frank Sinatra "It had to be you" cuts out into Metallica's "Enter Sandman" when headed up the lift hill. How cool is that?! It truly pumps you up for the experience or makes you more nervous than you were, to begin with. All in all, this is a must-ride in your lifetime. Add it to your bucket list and watch a POV of this one on YouTube.

Jurassic World Velocicoaster (Islands of Adventure, Florida)

Type: Steel

Model: LSM launched coaster

Height: 155'

Top Speed: 70 mph

Track Length: 4,700 ft.

Manufacturer: Intamin

The experience, yes, I'm calling it an experience, starts off with an elaborately themed queue line that will impress. You'll even head into a room where ultra-realistic velociraptor animatronics are in their stables. The ride itself is even better, though, and the theming doesn't quit once you make it onto the ride, unlike most attractions and especially roller coasters. Velociraptors are present throughout the ride experience, as well as landscaping and a complete set for the storyline, which puts riders right in the center of it. This Intamin steel multi-launched coaster hits a top speed with its second launch of 70 miles per hour. Its tallest point is a 155-foot top hat followed by a 140-foot drop. This ride also has some excellent standout inversions and elements, such as the "Mosasaurus Roll."

Tip 76: The Mosasaurus Roll is a whippy and (low to the water it sits above) heartline roll. Despite being a tight element, the ride vehicles whip through it at 53 miles per hour, which truly makes this its signature element.

The ride still, prior to this, has a superb set of overbank turns, speed hills (even an outer bank airtime hill), and three other inversions, such as the zero-G stall that shortly follows the major drop. This ride is raved about for its complete experience, which is why it should be easily added to your bucket list of must- rides.

Maverick (Cedar Point, Sandusky, Ohio)

Type: Steel

Model: Blitz

Height: 105'

Top Speed: 70 mph

Track Length: 4,450 ft.

Manufacturer: Intamin

This Intamin Blitz coaster (a model we don't see enough at parks) sits at just 105 feet tall. It's a mystery that such a short-standing ride packs such a punch, so I share how. An LSM lift hill (or some consider it to be a launch) starts the ride off with riders feeling that they already have a lack of control over what's about to happen. The first drop is 95 degrees beyond vertical, which leads to a series of bank turns, airtime hills, and a Twisted Horseshoe Roll.

Tip 77: A Twisted Horseshoe Roll is essentially a pair of corkscrews with a 180 turn around between the two.

This is eventually followed by a slowdown, in which riders find themselves in a tunnel with nothing but 400 feet of launch track ahead of them. You see where this is going, right? A 70-mile-per-hour launch is followed by a banked turn which leads to the final series of elements such as an S-curve, an airtime hill, and eventually the brake run. This ride is tight, whippy, and intense.

Tip 78: The ride initially had a heartline roll instead of its S curve, but the element was deemed too intense for riders and would put too much strain on the trains, so it was ultimately removed.

If I'm being honest, it's quite a bummer. Nevertheless, this ride is well worth a trip to Cedar Point, although Cedar Point is well worth a trip even without Maverick. Moral of the story: You should visit our number two pick, Cedar Point!

Fury 325 (Carowinds, South & North Carolina)

Type: Steel

Model: Giga

Height: 325'

Top Speed: 95 mph

Track Length: 6,602 ft.

Manufacturer: Bollinger & Mabillard

Tip 79: Here's a fun fact for you: this ride actually crosses through two states, both North and South Carolina.

Here's another fact, although it may be more of an opinion: This is probably the best Giga coaster built to date. Standing at 325 feet tall (I bet you didn't see that coming), this B&M Giga features a first drop that never seems to end. A series of overbanked curves, a 192-foot horseshoe element that will give riders a sensation that feels like it's defying the laws of gravity. Followed by an underground dive, a double helix, a barrel hill, and some camel-like airtime hills

that will give some of that classic sustained B&M floater airtime.
There is a myriad of excellent elements on the ride, and what
coaster enthusiasts rave about it is the fact that it holds its high
speed consistently through the course of the attraction. It tops out
at 95 miles per hour after the first drop, but each of its elements is
done at high speed, which truly makes this an intense coaster. Fury
325 is everything B&M does well with its Giga coaster models
packed into one coaster, which is why you should add Fury 325 to
your bucket list.

Intimidator 305

Type: Steel

Model: Giga

Height: 305 ft.

Top Speed: 90 mph

Track Length: 5,100 ft.

Manufacturer: Intamin

This ride may be too intense for not just some but many coaster
enthusiasts. Imagine going up a 305-foot lift hill, dropping 300 feet,
and instantly finding yourself going through a tight banked turn
immediately after hitting your top speed. As you'd imagine, it
causes frequent blackouts and riders to pass out. After all, you hit
90 miles per hour at the bottom of the first drop, and that banked
turn at the bottom seems to go on forever. But not in a sluggish
way, but more of a "your Dale Earnhardt going around a turn while
racing and you're in the passenger's seat bracing themselves and
waiting for the turn to be completed" way. Although the ride has a
few airtime hills, these are not the signature elements of the
coaster. Instead, the whippy laterals, turns, and curves, while going
at high speed, are what makes this ride unique and different for a

Giga coaster. The ride is focused on these sharp twists, which give the sensation that you are, in fact, in a race car. Before heading up the cable lift, you'll hear a recording that says, "Gentleman, start your engines!" This is followed by a revving noise, and then this insane, out-of-your-body roller coaster gets going. If you're okay with the possibility of graying or blacking out on a coaster that hits a sustained 4.5 G's, add this to your bucket list. It will not disappoint.

Tip 80: Do not ride this coaster on an empty stomach, and be hydrated before riding; otherwise, your chance of passing out on this coaster will increase.

The Voyage (Holiday World, Santa Claus, Indiana)

Type: Wood

Height: 159'

Top Speed: 67 mph

Track Length: 6,442 ft.

Manufacturer: Gravity Group

This wooden coaster is kind of insane; the ride has a combined 24.3 seconds of airtime altogether! This means *The Voyage* has more airtime to go around than any other ride in existence. Standing at 173 feet tall and having over 6,000 feet of track, this ride has nearly three minutes of ride time. It's long and relentless. It also has a series of 90-degree overbanked turns to add for good measure.

Tip 81: The Voyage also has more underground tunnels than any other coaster, with five of them.

This just makes for an even crazier night ride, which many consider the best time to ride *The Voyage*. Perhaps a night ride is what specifically you should put on your bucket list when you add this one to it.

El Toro (Six Flags Great Adventure, Jackson Township, New Jersey)

Type: Wood (prefabricated track)

Height: 181'

Top Speed: 70 mph

Track Length: 4,400 ft.

Manufacturer: Intamin

Depending on who you're asking, this prefabricated wooden coaster might be even more insane than *The Voyage*. El Toro may not be as long as a ride, but its airtime hills give some of the most incredible airtime on a coaster. I'm talking about some enormous ejector airtime hills, one after another. The coaster tops out at 70 miles per hour, which is incredibly fast for a wooden coaster, and it sits at 181 feet tall. It has an out-and-back layout, and it's definitely worth visiting Six Flags Great Adventure just to ride this beast of a wooden coaster.

Iron Gwazi (Busch Gardens Tampa, Tampa, Florida)

Type: Steel hybrid

Height: 206'

Top Speed: 76 mph

Track Length: 4,075 ft.

Manufacturer: Rocky Mountain Construction

Either this ride or the next RMC that we'll be introducing could easily be considered the most intense RMC built thus far. Iron Gwazi has a beyond vertical drop that leads straight from one overwhelming element to the next. It has elements such as a zero-G stall, ejector airtime hills, and over-banked curves, as it whips riders through these elements while maintaining excellent pacing. Its signature element is easily the "Death roll" or the "Barrel Roll Down Drop."

Tip 82: This element has gone viral for how crazy it appears just to the eye alone. Basically, it does what the second and more official name I offered for it was. It's a barrel roll that is simultaneously dropping you. The element itself is also very whippy and sudden, which adds to the intensity factor.

I suggest checking out a short clip of just this element alone. RMCs are great at being consistent and giving unique sensations that push the envelope of what type of elements can be done on roller coasters, and this fact is truly embodied with Iron Gwazi. The trains also look super cool on this thing. Check pictures of them out on google images or ride this thing for yourself and see... which is me inferring to add this to your bucket list!

Expedition G-Force (Holiday Park, Germany)

Type: Steel

Model: Mega

Height: 174'

Top Speed: 74 mph

Track Length: 4,002 ft.

Manufacturer: Intamin

This ride, from the get-go, has a unique first drop that includes two semi-twists that change directions. From there, riders will experience a series of large hills that give excellent airtime as well as overbanked turns. As the name suggests, riders will experience a point of 4.5 G's on the coaster, meaning that Expedition G-Force does an excellent job at giving riders both the sensations of negative and positive G's.

Tip 83: Another fun fact about this ride is that the game Roller Coaster Tycoon 3 has this as a pre-built ride, anyone else grow up playing that game? I sure did.

The scenery around the ride is also beautiful, and it just does a perfect job of executing what its elements intend to do. The ride always ranks high up in the Golden Ticket Award's top steel coasters for a good reason.

Zadra (Energylandia, Poland)

Type: Steel hybrid

Height: 200'

Top Speed: 75 mph

Track Length: 4,318 ft.

Manufacturer: Rocky Mountain Construction

If Iron Gwazi isn't someone's favorite RMC, perhaps it may be Zadra. Zadra has incredible elements such as its Twisted top hat, its zero-G stall, as well as its step-up under flip.

Tip 84: The step-up under flip is a unique element in which riders will go up a hill into a 270 degrees roll followed by a drop off to the side.

This element will throw you one way, upside, into another; it's a rather whippy element that throws you in different directions. Everything is to a major scale on this ride, which left room for RMC to create their typical classic RMC elements that all have loved to come and enjoy but have blown them up into larger versions of those elements. Zadra is another must-ride that should be added to your bucket list.

The Smiler (Alton Towers, United Kingdom)

Type: Steel

Model: Infinity

Height: 98'

Top Speed: 53 mph

Track Length: 3,828 ft.

Manufacturer: Gerstlauer

This coaster has the record for most inversions in a roller coaster, coming set with a whopping 14 of them. Despite this, the scariest or (might I say) creepiest aspect of this ride has to be the theming it possesses. The centerpiece to the ride is this enormous set of screens with graphics, videos, and more; this centerpiece sits on five legs and is referred to as "The Marmaliser." In terms of the elements you'll experience, this ride has a pre-first lift-hill heartline roll right off the bat. After this, you'll discover this ride has two lift hills, the second being a vertical lift hill that comes after a good chunk of the ride. In addition, you'll experience corkscrews, double corkscrews, sidewinders, dive loops, and even a sea serpent.

Tip 85: A sea serpent is basically a cobra roll, but instead of returning back to where you came from, you maintain the same direction you enter in instead.

All in all, The Smiler is a unique ride. There is nothing else like it, so you should add this oddball coaster to your bucket list.

Starry Sky Ripper (World Joyland, China)

Type: Steel

Model: Flying

Height: 131'

Top Speed: 55 mph

Track Length: 2,805 ft.

Manufacturer: Bolliger & Mabillard

Like most flying coasters, the pretzel loop is the signature element. On this coaster, it does, in fact, have the pretzel loop in which riders dive head over heels to the point where they lay on their backs, but instead of coming back up, it flips riders back into the flying position through an overbanked turn. It's quite a brilliant transition. The coaster has a whopping five inversions, even including an inline twist and a zero-G roll. This is personally on my bucket list, too, being a flying coaster that is out of my reach of travel at the moment. For these reasons, please make riding this thing a priority on your bucket list, especially if you love flying coasters.

Other Honorable Mentions:

Obviously, we can only go in-depth with so many bucket list coasters, but I also wanted to give you a quick list of other ones you must consider. Here, I'll list the coaster, park, and one specific reason why you should add it to your bucket list. So here are our honorable mentions:

- *Kingda ka* **(Six Flags Great Adventure)**

Reason to ride: This is the tallest coaster in the world as it's a strata coaster that launches riders at 128 miles per hour and peaks at the height of 456 feet.

- *Formula Rossa* **(Ferrariland)**

Reason to ride: This is the fastest coaster in the world; it launches riders at 149 miles per hour!

- **Hakugei (Nagashima Spa Land)**

Reason to ride: This RMC hybrid competes with Iron Gwazi and Zadra (previously mentioned) as the best RMC out there, as this has a layout and airtime-filled elements that compete with the best.

- **Steel vengeance (Cedar Point)**

Reason to ride: This is another large-scale RMC hybrid with a second half that is better than the first! Some still consider this to be the best RMC, but those are typically people who regularly attend Cedar Point and believe this out of wishful thinking!

- **Lightning Rod (Dollywood)**

Reason to ride: It's the world's first wooden coaster with a launch, and it features incredible out-of-your-seat airtime, especially with its quadruple-down element.

Tip 86: A "double-down," "triple-down," or "quadruple-down" is essentially an airtime hill followed by more airtime hills in which once completing the first airtime hill, you go down the other airtime hills without going back up a hill. So basically, you keep experiencing the second half of a hill (going down) over and over and over and over again, which gives an incredible sensation of ejector airtime multiple times while already being ejected from your seat from the previous hill.

- **Do Dodonpa (Fuji Q-Highland)**

Reason to ride: It launches and reaches a speed of 112 miles per hour in just 1.5 seconds; just imagine how crazy that must feel.

- **Eejanaika (Fuji Q-Highland)**

Reason to ride: It's a 4D coaster, not the first, which is X2. Many argue it's smoother and has a better layout than X2, so I'd check this one out if it's possible if I were you.

- **Skyrush (Hersheypark)**

Reason to ride: This Intamin hyper coaster might be the most intense hyper coaster ever built; ride it for yourself to find out.

- **Montu (Busch Gardens, Tampa)**

Reason to ride: This is widely considered to be the best B&M invert ever built. It has the perfect layout for this type of ride model.

Obviously, there are many other coasters that I could've added to this list. In fact, I know I easily could have squeezed a few more RMCs there if I wanted to (*cough cough, Wildfire at Kolmarden and Outlaw Run at Silver Dollar City*). Nevertheless, I highly recommend adding each of these coasters to your bucket list roller coasters if, in fact, that is a list you are currently creating.

Chapter 5: World-class attractions (that aren't roller coasters) that you should also add to the bucket list

I get it; not everyone is a coaster enthusiast. And that's okay! There is a reason parks are always looking to diversify the types of rides and attractions they have to offer to guests because, just like every other aspect of life, people have different tastes. Therefore, let's go through rides that are bucket list worthy that aren't exactly roller coasters. Starting with:

Flat rides

Both the Haunted Mine Drop and Giant Canyon Swing (Glenwood Caverns, Colorado)

I previously mentioned Glenwood Caverns since it did, in fact, find itself high up on the HowExpert Guide list of the top 101 amusement parks to visit. Haunted Mine Drop is a unique drop tower that (the way I see it) has similar theming to that of a haunted mansion, except it's a haunted cavern. The drop catches riders by surprise as they drop in pitch black. As for Giant Canyon Swing, I briefly shared a bit about it earlier. But to refresh, it essentially is a Screamin' Swing model that sits off the edge of a cliff, and I'm sure you could imagine what that means. Both attractions can only be experienced at Glenwood Caverns, which makes them a must add to your bucket list.

I also would like to acknowledge and honor the death of the young 6-year-old female guest that lost her life in a tragic accident at the Haunted Mine Drop attraction in September of 2021. My thoughts and prayers go out to all affected by the incident. It's a saddening incident to which I would like to pay my respects, especially considering that this book was written not too long after the incident occurred.

Gravity Bomb (Bigfoot on the Strip)

This ride is quite terrifying. This is another drop tower that sits 200 feet above the ground. You initially slowly head up the tower, just like any other drop tower. Then you drop. What else did you expect? It's a drop tower, after all. The missing aspect of this ride is that you are held by just a seat belt. No over-the-shoulder restraints and no lap bar. Just a measly little seatbelt. This is definitely a ride that is for thrill seekers that are looking to push to the edge.

The Stratosphere (all the rides)

Right in the heart of Las Vegas sits this stupidly insane building. With a set of three flat rides, each individually finding ways to psych guests out into thinking they're going to die, it's no question that if that's your kind of thrill, a trip to Las Vegas may be your next move. The first flat ride I'll share about it is *Big Shot*. *Big Shot* is a launched drop tower, so it shoots you up an already 921-foot platform (the building itself) and leaves you up to almost 1,100 feet in the air until plummeting back down. Although, in my opinion, this may be the most intense flat ride that sits at the top of the building, it is not the most terrifying. For instance, there's *X-Scream*. *X-Scream* literally totters riders over the edge of the structure, which is well over 800 feet in the atmosphere. How far over the edge, you might ask? 27 feet. Yep, 27 feet off the edge of an over 800-foot ledge. The ride itself is not special; in fact, this ride model is often seen in the kid's section of the park at your typical amusement or theme park. It's truly just the height and scare factor of being 800 feet off the ground that makes this attraction so ridiculous.

Last but not least, *Insanity* is their other crazy contraption that sits atop The Stratosphere. This ride has an arm that extends over 60 feet off the edge of the building, in which little pods that sit two riders spin around off the edge of the building while simultaneously being turned towards to ground at a 70 degrees angle--all while pulling a good amount of G's while spinning. Many consider *this* to be the most intense and terrifying attraction, although you may just need to ride these rides to find out for yourself.

Tower of Terror (various Disney parks)

Okay, so maybe the one at California Adventure is now themed to Guardians of the Galaxy, but it's not quite the same classic Tower of Terror that a lot of us grew up to love. Don't get me wrong, Guardians of the Galaxy is awesome. The ride has more drops and seems to provide more action, and the music and lively atmosphere make it plenty of fun. But for those still themed to Tower of Terror, we are thankful that the nostalgic attraction lives on. With an eerie hotel queue that sets the tone, guests are invited into this haunted-looking Hollywood hotel building. Themed to *The Twilight Zone,* guests are shown a pre-show of a rainy night in 1939 Hollywood. A bolt of lightning strikes the hotel, and a family dissipates while they ride the elevator. The elevator is what the riders themselves board, and the narrator in the pre-show suggests that the riders are next. For the ride experience itself, riders head through a series of scenes in which the riders enter *The Twilight Zone* or the Fifth Dimension. Following this, riders go through the drop sequence, going up lifts and down drops.

Tip 87: There are four different, randomized sequences riders may experience. This adds to the re-rideability factor of the attraction.

So there you have it, this is a fan-favorite of many, whether at Hollywood Studios in Florida, Walt Disney Studios park in Paris, or Tokyo Disneysea.

Honorable Mentions:

Well, there are a few honorable mentions I could share. *Zumanjaro Drop of Doom* is the world's tallest drop tower as it's attached to *Kingda Ka*, the world's tallest coaster. I'd also mention that the giant large frisbee pendulum rides are a must if you find yourself at a park with one. Manufacturers seem to be getting increasingly creative and innovative with their concepts of flat rides, so I'd also like to remind you to keep an eye open as to what's next!

Water Rides

Not to be confused with water coasters, which seem to be getting more popular for large, chained parks to be added, water rides (as we touched base upon earlier) are either usually log flumes or rapids rides. Here are a few bucket list water rides to be noted:

Splash Mountain (various Disney parks)

Chances are, you've probably ridden one of the Splash Mountains before. Splash Mountain is a timeless classic that is a generational favorite. With its classic, Brer Rabbit, at the time of this being written, the parks are seemingly going to be retheming Splash Mountain to Princess and the Frog. Either way, whether you ride it with Brer Rabbit, or Princess Tiana, this ride will be filled with color, animatronics, and a series of drops, including the classic "big-take-your-photo-and-scream-drop" at the end. So, for nostalgic purposes, everyone should ride Splash Mountain at some point in their life.

Timber Mountain Log Ride (Knott's Berry Farm)

Right in the center of their historic Ghost Town sits one of the oldest operating log flumes rides to exist. This historic ride, opening in 1969, should be added to your bucket list simply for historical purposes. The mountain itself is actually 320 feet long, as riders weave in and out through the mountain and different scenes. Like most great log flumes, this one ends with its classic free fall, followed by a splashdown. The ride now has updated animatronics as well, which is good considering how little advanced they were back in the 1900s. Overall, this ride is one of, if not the best, log flumes to ride. The only flume that I might just choose above this one would have to be what's next.

Chiapas (Phantasialand)

This ride is manufactured by Intamin, who we have consistently been raving about with their incredible steel beasts of roller coasters.

Tip 88: This log flume actually boasts the steepest drop on a log flume, which is not surprising considering Inatamin did, in fact, design the ride.

The drop also happens to be 66 feet. The flume sits in the Mexican-themed area of the park and has not just excellent landscaping but also excellent Aztec theming and special effects (colored lighting, fog, etc.). The log flume also has two track changes, so yes, it does, in fact, go backward as well. The log flume ends with its final drop, followed by a camel hill before its final splashdown. This is easily the most ambitious log flume to exist to date, which is why I see it as a must-add to your bucket list.

Valhalla (Blackpool Pleasure Beach)

This log flume is entirely indoors, which makes it quite intriguing for guests who have never written it before. The ride has a very long ride time as well, over six minutes, which means that it may be fair to even wait in a long line for this attraction. The ride is themed to the Vikings and takes riders through a long series of scenes in which they appropriately ride in a Viking Ship flume. Viking chanting music plays throughout the ride. Also: this ride will soak you. As this book is being written, it also appears that the ride is under refurbishment, which means new set pieces or effects may or may not be added. Still nevertheless, this will enhance the ride experience that already comes with fire, fog, and all sorts of lighting. If you are a fan of fun and interesting log flumes, then this ride is most certainly one to add to your bucket list.

One more honorable mention: For another honorable mention, I don't have any specific ride at a park to shout out. But I have a must-do experience that may be the most fun you ever have at an amusement park. Many parks do have a rapid ride in which six riders sit in a round raft facing each other as they rip through a course of water.

Tip 89: The rapids are created through logs or tubes, which disrupt the normal flow of water. Here, the raft will hit the waves created and make the large splashes that soak you and your friends.

Going on these attractions with people you know, and sharing a laugh, is quite possibly one of my favorite experiences at a park. So what I suggest as a must-ride to add to your bucket list is to get on one of these things with a group of friends and spend the time laughing at the friend sitting next to you that happened to get way more soaked than you. Or maybe you're *that* friend...

Dark Rides

Here's the last category that we haven't yet been able to cover. These dark rides go above and beyond with their special effects, well-detailed queue lines, and an unforgettable ride experience that drives lines past the three-hour mark. Well, forget that last part. Get a fast pass.

Harry Potter and the Forbidden Journey (various Universal parks)

Keep in mind that upon entering the queue for this ride, riders are already immersed in the *Wizarding World of Harry Potter*. Sitting in Hogwarts Castle, the centerpiece of the entire land and quite a magnificent structure to marvel at. After a series of hallways and replica rooms of the castle, riders find themselves ready to ride. Depending on how much of a Harry Potter fan you are will impact how easily you will be able to follow it. The ride vehicles themselves have all sorts of functionality to them as you sit on the "enchanted benches." Riders will spin, ride on their back, twist, and drop. They have over-the-shoulder restraints for this reason. The ride utilizes both animatronics (very impressive ones, I might add), as well as simulation and wrap-around projection screens. The most impressive piece this ride has to offer is the animatronic dragon (which literally does breathe on you with fire). Riders will also find themselves in the Forbidden Forest, where nearly an equally impressive willow swipes at riders and sends them to the Quidditch Pitch.

All in all, the storyline is well executed, as riders are quite literally at the center of it all. The effects, animatronics, and overall production are impressive, and it's something you'll have to experience for yourself. This attraction should be at the top of your bucket list if you are a Harry Potter fan.

Rise of the Resistance (various Disney parks)

This ride is the most impressive and highly technical piece of art ever to be created. Located in the highly detailed and immersive *Star Wars Galaxy Edge*, Rise of the Resistance is more than just a ride. The line queue alone is worth waiting for. First, guests enter as new recruits in which BB-8 and a Rey hologram have a mission for riders. Then they enter a CEC Transportation ship, and quite literally, they board one, as they are eventually attacked and ultimately captured by a Star Destroyer. Then guests exit the ship and find themselves in a hangar bay with lines and rows of stormtroopers on display. What's cool is the structure itself sways and gives the impression to guests that they are on an actual ship. The employees working the line are also taking things seriously, as they are both guiding you through the line while simultaneously being actors through and through.

Once riders get in their escape pod, which travels without a track as this is, in fact, a trackless dark ride, they go through a series of rooms and scenes that are nothing short of incredible and awe-inspiring. Specific moments make you wonder how such real-looking animatronics or forms of action could even be possible, like the part in which Kylo Ren's lightsaber actually cuts through the ceiling. At the same time, you escape, or the large-scale AT-ATs cause riders to marvel. This ride is quite versatile as you lift, spin, and vibrate through the course. I must mention that the special effects are incredibly executed. At the end of the ride, riders find themselves in a motion simulator in which the pods eject, which they actually do so down with a vertical drop track. This is where the final scene occurs before the escape pods bring you to the end of the ride. As you can tell, I am also choosing not to spoil the experience too much for those who are planning to ride the attraction. This ride is an incredible mark of history for Disney and the industry as a whole, as it marks a new level of innovation. As I mentioned, it is widely considered to be the most advanced attraction ever to exist to date. For all these reasons, even for non-Star Wars fans, this must be on your bucket list of attractions to experience.

20,000 Leagues Under The Sea

Okay, so maybe any other dark ride we discuss may not be as technologically advanced as the one we just talked about, but there are still some incredible world-class attractions that I'd love to share with you. 20,000 Leagues Under The Sea is a beautiful submarine dark ride based on Jules Verne's novel of the same name. The storyline is as follows: riders are essentially taking a tour of the world under the sea. But when Captain Nemo fails to levitate the vehicle, a Kraken attacks the submarine as riders find themselves in an unknown world in which these mermen eventually help you find your way back to the base. That sounds a bit like a drug-filled Indie rock music video but believe me when I say that once you ride this attraction, it'll be a cohesive and thrilling storyline to be thrust into. The sets and scenes are absolutely gorgeous. The special effects are second to none.

Tip 90: Bubble effects in the window of the submarine that the riders are looking through give the impression to riders that they are actually underwater; however, the sets and scenes are not actually underwater.

Leave it to Disney to continually innovate in such ways, even in 2001 when this attraction was opened to the public.

Symbolica (Efteling)

This trackless dark ride is centered around this figure, King Pardulfus until another character by the name of Pardoes (the jester) gives riders a tour of the palace in parts they weren't necessarily expecting to see. What's unique about this ride is that there are 11 different scenes with three routes covering nine of the 11 scenes. This, of course, adds to the re-rideability factor. The ride even lasts about seven minutes, which is hopefully enough time for the rider to soak in the beauty and detail of each scene within the palace that is displayed. Some scenes even allow the riders to use the interactive features shown in front of them, such as controlling the musical sounds in the music lounge (Muziek Salon) scene. All in all, this craft and the neat dark ride have nothing but rave reviews. You should add it to your bucket list for this reason.

Darren Brown's Ghost Train (Thorpe Park)

Here is quite possibly the most unique and the most daunting attraction to be mentioned. This may also be a controversial pick, considering that the ride doesn't always receive the most positive attention. The attraction as a whole combines live action, virtual reality, and typical dark ride elements. Let's just say it isn't for everyone in terms of the ride experience and what it encompasses.

Tip 91: Kids under the age of 13 are discouraged from riding because of the "extreme psychological nature" that the attraction possesses.

I won't try to spoil too much for this ride, and if I'm being honest, this ride is geared towards your first experience because it relies heavily on the element of surprise, especially jump scares. I'd also add that it relies heavily on optical illusions and confusing guests with what exactly is going on. Derren Brown is present throughout the experience, and he suggests that you (the rider) may have an altered perspective or relationship with fear once the attraction is over. To give a brief run through of this attraction, you enter a pre-show in which Derren Brown introduces the ghost train. Afterward, you head into a room where an apparently suspended train sits lifted by chains. Guests enter this train, in which they begin the first VR portion of the attraction. This is followed by a live-action section in which riders get out of their pod, which is no longer the train they entered, and then following the live-action portion of the ride; they get back in to finish off the last VR portion of the ride. Afterward, guests exit into the gift shop, but there is one last surprise. If you plan on riding this attraction, skip the rest of this paragraph because it does contain spoilers. Here's what happens: once all the guests arrive in the gift shop, there is a final jumpscare in which the lights flicker, and a demon (which is someone in a costume) jumps out and scares everyone. So while people are just assuming they are in the typical cash-grab gift shop that's at the end of every ride, they are in for a treat. A terrifying one!

All in all, many suggest that how well the ride's special effects and VR work will impact whether you have a "good ride" on this attraction or not. Nevertheless, this controversial ride is worth checking out. That's why I have included it here.

Honorable Mentions:

Pirates of the Caribbean (various Disney parks)

Reason to ride: It's a timeless Disney classic, and it still presents some incredible-looking scenes to go along with the storyline.

Amazing Adventure of Spider-Man (Universal Studios, Orlando)

Reason to ride: This one is still seen as the gold standard for modern dark rides, despite opening up back in 1999. There is no question that this attraction was ahead of its time, combining physical sets and 3D motion simulator elements as well.

Journey to the Center of the Earth (Tokyo Disneysea)

Reason to ride: This dark ride actually hits 47 miles per hour, with similar mechanics to that of Test Track at Epcot. Riders board these interesting-looking mining cars as they travel through beautiful looking caverns until a giant earthquake disrupts all of it; this is where the thrills begin...

Flight of Passage (Disney's Animal Kingdom)

Reason to ride: Some actually argue this to be their favorite theme park attraction altogether, for a good reason. This elaborately done 3D flying motion simulator takes riders on a journey across Pandora's landscape through a storyline that's worth investing yourself into. Also, the line queue to this thing is so well done, to the extent that you'll enjoy waiting in that portion of the queue.

All in all, each of these attractions is not just tier one within their category of the ride. They also happen to be pushing the envelope for what manufacturers, Imagineers, and ride developers can create and execute. They are nothing short of world-class, and they deserve to have long lines (yes, I said it). That's why each of these rides (even the honorable mentions) should be added to your bucket list.

Chapter 6: Other Aspects of Theme Parks

When working on the list of the best 101 parks around the world, it's definitely easy to consider the rides themselves. But what truly gives the complete experience is when a park can deliver on all fronts, including having good food, clean bathrooms, and quality entertainment. So in this next chapter, we'll be reviewing some of the other important aspects of theme parks.

Food

This is a make-or-break for many visitors. Attending a theme or amusement park definitely helps when there is a variety of foods. Is this just another American theme park that can't help but serve pizza, chicken, hot dogs, and burgers? Or do they also offer Mexican food, Chinese cuisine, and a bakery that serves the best cinnamon bread?

Tip 92: Dollywood has the best cinnamon bread at an amusement park; go and try it if you ever get the chance to visit the park!

You see, food is rather important. From my own personal experience, the Disney, Universal, and Merlin Entertainment Parks tend to do the best job delivering quality meals. Also, from my own personal experience, Six Flags easily does the worst job of providing quality meals.

We are also at a point within the industry where food is overpriced, whether you eat at Six Flags or Disneyland. There is no cheaper chain; after all, I've recently had to pay $13 for some chicken tenders and fries at Magic Mountain. That's why I suggest this:

Tip 93: If you are attending a park for an extended stay or happen to be a pass holder, you will want to check out the Dining Meal Plans that parks often offer. It will save you money. Tip: Also, the souvenir bottles are a worth it investment because the whole family can share and have unlimited Sprite and Coke, especially if you are a season pass holder.

Although how tasty food is can be rather subjective, it will definitely impact your time at a park. That's why it's something to consider before heading to one of them, although, in my opinion, it's never a good deciding factor. And remember

Tip 94: If a park does not allow outside food and beverage, smuggle some snacks in your jacket or sweatshirt and stuff that into your bag. It will pass through the security check with no problem and works like a charm.

And quite frankly, I've had bag checkers crunch chips through my bed and not care, they still let me in, and I had some yummy Sour Cream and Onion Lays to snack on while in line for one of the rides.

Shows

This seems to be a category that most chains actually tend to do a great job in. Often, hidden gems within a park are shows. They can be entertaining, thrilling, or even educational. My personal favorite show at a theme park would definitely have to be Water World at Universal Studios Hollywood. That's because I'm a sucker for action, stunts, and getting wet.

But obviously the different types of parks you will attend will have different types of shows. For example, Disney parks will have theatrical Disney-related entertainment, as well as fireworks and parades.

Tip 95: If you hate waiting on Main Street for parades while the rest of your family eagerly sits on the curb two hours early... well, sorry, I have no tip for you there. You're sort of out of luck.

Disney will usually have some excellent shows as well. Now, if it happens to be an animal park, the shows will either be the animals and trainers putting on a presentation or a giant whale splashing everyone.

Tip 96: You hopefully have a poncho on and ready to keep you somewhat dry.

If you attend a Universal Park, the shows will have high-quality productions and often may even be thrilling or filled with stunts. If you attend a Merlin Park, it really depends on the specific park you are attending. From my understanding, their parks tend to have very traditional types of shows with good quality actors and talents, especially if the show contains any dancing.

Be sure to check out the shows and showtimes before heading to a park if that happens to be something you are interested in. Personally, I've never been much of a show fan because rides are truly where you can get an experience that is unlike anything else. But not everyone is wired the same, or like me, so shows may very well be something you'll want to consider before heading to the park.

Tip 97: Back to Disneyland (and Disneyland specifically); if you want to watch the firework show but leave at a reasonable time, the firework show is still excellent from the parking structure. In fact, you may even be closer to the fireworks. You'll just miss out on the music and other special effects that take place on Main Street, but you will also miss out on the hour-long tram lines that take you back to the parking structure once the show is finished.

Water Parks

I could write a whole separate book about water parks, especially since they attract so many guests yearly. However, water parks are in their own category, separate from the theme and amusement parks. There are different slide types, models, and structures. There are lazy rivers and giant wave pools. They as well have food and atmosphere to be concerned about. That's why I have decided to remain more on topic with amusement parks and theme parks in this book because diving into the waters with this topic would most certainly be a rabbit hole.

Most Six Flags and Cedar Fair Parks do offer water parks next door. They will typically come set with a selection of thrilling slides, especially the ones with trap doors in which the floor drops from beneath the guest and family slides. These tend to be raft slides that can fit two to four riders.

Disney and Universal do an excellent job theming their water parks. Volcano *Bay* in Orlando is worth mentioning as it has an enormous volcano at the centerpiece of the park.

There are also chains and parks that are completely removed from the rest of the amusement park industry that just own the water parks. For example, *Village Roadshow Theme Parks and ERP Properties* own all the various Wet n' Wild water parks.

All in all, it would be no surprise that the more theming an amusement park may have, would suggest that the same would translate over the water park. So be sure to keep that in mind.

Meet n' greets!

This is present with most parks, and it ultimately depends on which type of park you're going to. Obviously, a Nickelodeon-themed park likely has closets full of SpongeBob costumes. However, if you find yourself taking little ones to the park, you'll likely spend just as much time waiting for rides as you will for your kids to meet Mickey Mouse. Nevertheless, this is an aspect of parks to keep in mind before you visit.

Tip 98: Many of the characters will be able to sign autographs. If you are bringing any kids, it's always fun to take them to the gift shop to grab an autograph book as they then try to gather as many autographs from different characters as they can.

This is especially true if you happen to be a season pass holder at your local park, then the kids will have multiple trips and opportunities in that instance.

Chapter 7: The Visit Itself!

At this point, you've learned pretty much all there is to know about the amusement/theme park industry. You have background knowledge of all the different types of rides, what they do, and what their objective is. You have a basic understanding of the different types of roller coasters, what makes each model and manufacturer unique, and all the different coaster enthusiast terminology that will help you fit in with the cool kids. But now it's time to actually visit the park. Using our top 101 list, you likely have picked out a park that is within a reasonable distance of you. Now what? What more could you do to prepare for your visit, and what is there to expect? That's what this last chapter is here for.

How to Prepare for your Visit

I'll do this section by giving you a list of things to do to prepare for your visit. Each of these is beneficial and will help your day at the park run as smoothly as possible:

- **Check the weather before you go**

Even before you create your list of essentials to bring, it is pivotal that you know what conditions you are getting yourself into. For example, should you pack a rain poncho or umbrella? Or should you pack light clothing? Will you need a jacket after sunset? Will you need any plastic bags to keep valuables from getting wet? Or will you need extra sunscreen? Keep all these types of questions in mind depending on the weather conditions for you on the day of your visit.

- **Create a list of essentials you'll need to bring**

Example:

- Water (Reusable bottle, parks often won't allow an opened plastic bottle)

- Snacks
- Sunscreen
- Sunglasses
- Sweatshirt (for when it cools off at night)
- Spending money (for souvenirs)
- Camera
- Backpack
- Lip balm
- Medication
- Phone charger
- Rain poncho
- Stroller
- First aid kit
- Hand Sanitizer

Of course, if you'd like to use this list as a reference, I see it as pretty complete.

- **Research the park and what your priorities are beforehand**

One of the worst things that can happen is walking through the entrance and having no idea which attraction you want to ride the most, or worse: which attractions are even at the park. Be sure to have a list of attractions that you most want to experience and make them a priority once you get through the gates.

Tip 99: In this instance, get to the park before the gates open and head right to the ride or attraction you desire to get on the most first. Chances are other visitors will also have the same attraction at the top of their list, so get in line before the line is too long!

Also, have a basic understanding of what the crowds may be like. There is a difference between a Saturday in July and a Tuesday in

February. Have realistic expectations of how large the crowds are going to be.

Tip 100: My recommendation is to visit on a non-peak day. For the best experience, choose a weekday to visit in a lower attendance part of the season for the park. Each park is different, so do your research for when that is!

- **Have a gameplan**

Plan as much out as possible and schedule certain parts of your day.

Tip 101: Sometimes, it's smart to get in line for a ride right before the park closes. This way, you extend your stay and don't mind waiting in a long line. It's an easy way to maximize your day.

Have a good idea of where your party will want to eat, what kind of pace they'll want to go at, and keep things to schedule as best as possible. This sort of is an extension of the last tip but be sure to have a plan beyond just the rides and attractions that are your priorities. Just be sure to not over plan things to where you are so focused on a schedule that you forget you're at an amusement park to just have a fun time with your friends or family!

- **Have fun**

Chances are, this is a day you'll be back at, in the future, as a sweet memory. Cherish the quality time you have with loved ones or friends, and be sure not to set too high of expectations for the day. Just let loose and enjoy yourself!

Tip 102: If there is a ride that you are hesitant to ride because it may be too scary or thrilling, those tend to be the best experiences, and I strongly recommend you ride it. There is a freedom in understanding that any ride you board will not last forever.

Parking

This is an unpopular topic. However, parks often charge a lot for you to park, sometimes up to $25 depending on where you go. This is why it helps to be a season pass holder, as in some instances, the season pass will allow you to bypass paying to park.

Tip 103: If a season pass perk is free parking but it takes an upgraded pass to get this perk, I recommend getting the more expensive pass if you plan to attend the park numerous times. It'll save money in the long run and also give you a pass that has more perks and possibly discounts.

Juggling Budget

My heart goes out to college students; not only are they broke, but they typically desire to go out and have the most fun simultaneously. It's not an easy life out there, folks! However, if parks are too expensive for you or your party, there are a few ways around this.

Tip 104: Some parks give military discounts; if anyone in your family served, they may be in luck!

Tip 105: Some parks have canned food drives; this is a fun way to get a free ticket if your local park does, in fact, offer this.

Tip 106: Always check in for promotions on sites like Groupon. Costco (for you Americans) is another great place to look as well. There are always sources that sell discounted tickets; you just have to search them out.

Hotels and Resorts

This very much depends on what type of visit you're making. If, in fact, you're visiting a park over the course of a vacation, or if it is, in fact, your vacation, definitely look into the hotel and resort options that the park has.

Tip 107: If possible, it may be cheaper to choose an off-site hotel, but the con is that it makes your stay less convenient.

In a sense, it's all about preference and whether you favor budget or the experience.

Conclusion:

Wow! That was a lot of information to take in. I suggest using this book as a guide, not just a one-time read-through. It's always helpful to have this information on hand. Now that you have all the background information needed to become a park expert and you're ready to pack up and head to the park, it appears here that my job is done. Be sure to have a good time at the park and to continue to ask questions and wonder how engineers and Imagineers alike are able to create such creative masterpieces and attractions. Continue to learn how Disney uses forced perspective in their parks or how RMC utilizes the pre-existent wooden supports in their hybrid coasters. There is a never-ending fountain of knowledge out there for those interested in this industry and how it operates, even down to each support's nails and bolts. With all this being said, it's been a pleasure going on this journey with you. And I hope to see you and your party at a park soon.

About the Author

Noah Granger, born and raised in Los Angeles, California, grew up surrounded by a plethora of amusement parks. From going to Disneyland on a weekly basis to conquering all the intimidating roller coasters of Six Flags Magic Mountain by the time he was a teenager; Noah developed a passion for this niche topic and an addiction to the adrenaline that he often got while riding Xcelerator at Knott's Berry Farm. Currently, a student at California State University Fullerton, Noah is continuously keeping up to date with all there is going on in the amusement and theme park industry. Over the years of learning more about this hobby, he has accumulated years and years' worth of knowledge surrounding all the different types of parks and thrill rides. What Noah cherishes most, though, are the friends and family that he gets to spend quality time with, standing in lines while at the parks. Luke 17:6

HowExpert publishes quick how to guides on all topics from A to Z by everyday experts. Visit HowExpert.com to learn more.

About the Publisher

Byungjoon "BJ" Min is an author, publisher, and founder of HowExpert. He started with a dream to make money online while in college. Like most, he failed and gave up on his dream to settle for a job as a convenience store clerk. However, he hated his job so much that he decided to go for his dreams one more time, and that decision made all the difference. Eventually, he did become a fulltime internet marketer and found his niche in publishing. The mission for HowExpert is to discover, empower, and maximize everyday people's talents to ultimately make a positive impact in the world for all topics from A to Z. Visit BJMin.com and HowExpert.com to learn more. John 14:6

Recommended Resources

- HowExpert.com – Quick 'How To' Guides on All Topics from A to Z by Everyday Experts.
- HowExpert.com/free – Free HowExpert Email Newsletter.
- HowExpert.com/books – HowExpert Books
- HowExpert.com/courses – HowExpert Courses
- HowExpert.com/clothing – HowExpert Clothing
- HowExpert.com/membership – HowExpert Membership Site
- HowExpert.com/affiliates – HowExpert Affiliate Program
- HowExpert.com/jobs – HowExpert Jobs
- HowExpert.com/writers – Write About Your #1 Passion/Knowledge/Expertise & Become a HowExpert Author.
- HowExpert.com/resources – Additional HowExpert Recommended Resources
- YouTube.com/HowExpert – Subscribe to HowExpert YouTube.
- Instagram.com/HowExpert – Follow HowExpert on Instagram.
- Facebook.com/HowExpert – Follow HowExpert on Facebook.
- TikTok.com/@HowExpert – Follow HowExpert on TikTok.